Person and Community

Person and Community

A Philosophical Exploration

edited by
ROBERT J. ROTH, S.J.

NEW YORK
FORDHAM UNIVERSITY PRESS
1975

Printed in the United States of America

To our teacher, friend, and colleague

JOSEPH DONCEEL, S.J.

Professor Emeritus of Philosophy, Fordham University.

For over thirty years, Professor Donceel has lectured and written on the theme of this book, and from him we have learned the philosophical meaning of person. These essays presuppose his work and attempt to extend it. But most of all, he has shown us how to live as persons. His kindness, priestly love, and openness to dialogue have helped us to become a genuine community of friends and scholars.

THE CONTRIBUTORS

W. Norris Clarke, s.j. Professor
Fordham University

John Donnelly Assistant Professor
Fordham University

Leonard C. Feldstein Associate Professor
Fordham University

Robert O. Johann Professor
Fordham University

Elizabeth M. Kraus Associate Professor
Fordham University

Quentin Lauer, s.j. Professor
Fordham University

Gerald A. McCool, s.j. Professor
Fordham University

Robert J. Roth, s.j. Professor
Fordham University
Dean of Fordham College

Aldo Tassi Associate Professor
Loyola College, Baltimore

CONTENTS

Preface

Robert J. Roth, s.j.

It was the Socratic turn which directed the attention of Western thought to man, focusing especially on the intellectual and moral dimensions peculiar to him, instead of considering him as merely another piece in the material cosmos. Since then, man has been at the center of all philosophical speculation, for it is man alone who philosophizes, and it is largely about him that philosophical questions revolve.

And yet this philosophical study of man has undergone profound evolution from Socrates' day to our own. Classical Greek and medieval thinkers tended to develop their conceptions of man within a metaphysical context based on theories of substance and of some kind of radical dualism within the essence of man (spirit–body, form–matter). Later philosophical reflection has criticized this model as being too static and essentialistic. Man, it is said, is conceived as an immutable, self-enclosed essence isolated from the changing existential and historical relationships which determine, condition, and alter both man's nature in the concrete and his view of the universe.

Whether or not such criticism is wholly justified, it is true that post-medieval philosophy has developed the position that man's nature and his view of himself and of the world about him cannot be adequately understood apart from (1) the constantly changing environment in which man lives, and (2) the communal relationships which exist between persons. In fact, many argue that man as person is what he is, and can be understood as such, only in terms of these changing conditions and interpersonal relationships.

It is upon this problem that the essays of the present volume focus. The contributors represent a variety of philosophical traditions, and they have been asked to express what contribution these traditions can make to our understanding of man and person.

To be sure, all of them are well aware of the responses which the Greeks and the Middle Ages made to this question; they are also familiar with the problems which contemporary philosophy has raised regarding the importance of relationships in understanding reality. Hence, from their own perspectives they have attempted to point out the philosophical considerations which must be included in any attempt to articulate a view of man and person meaningful for contemporary philosophy.

What has emerged is a series of essays on various aspects of the person and of his relation to community. The essays dialogue, as it were, with problems raised by Kant, Freud, Dewey, Whitehead, Skinner, Lonergan, Rahner, Macmurray, Rawls, and analytic philosophers. The philosophical issues are those involved in epistemology, social change, community, religion, moral commitment, political theory, peace, immortality, and technology. Surely there are other philosophers and philosophical issues which would have to be considered for a final synthesis regarding person. It would be difficult, however, to find within the pages of a single volume a greater variety of viewpoints bearing upon this most important theme.

The theme we have chosen is indeed timely, for, in an age of bewildering change and frightening insecurity, the meaning of person becomes a crucial one. Moreover, all the contributors have given serious consideration to the question of person in their lectures, courses, and publications. This enterprise has afforded us many hours of philosophical stimulation, insight, and enjoyment. It is our hope that we can share some of this with the readers of the present volume.

Person and Community

Philosophy and Social Change

Quentin Lauer, s.j.

It requires no great perspicacity on the part of the philosopher (or, for that matter, the non-philosopher) to recognize that the age in which we live is one of extraordinary changes and that those changes have had and are having an as yet uncalculated impact on the way men live their lives. Nonetheless, it does take more than ordinary discernment to evaluate both the changes and the impact they make. It can be said, of course, that in the dynamics of history any age is necessarily a period of change; but it is also true that one age more than another will in the course of history constitute a particularly significant turning point in the ongoing process of human living. There are periods in history when the forces of change are concentrated in such a way that the periods in question stand out as milestones on man's pathway through time. What characterizes our present age is not only that it is one of those milestones, one of those points in which the energies of change are concentrated, but also that at present the tempo of change has been accelerated to a degree unprecedented in past history.

The rapidity of contemporary change is such that, before we can become effectively adjusted to one change, another has supervened to challenge our adjustability even more. It is, in fact, precisely this factor of adjustability which makes today's "generation gap" so poignant; it is far easier to adjust to change when what is faced is not recognized as change but only as the way things are. One generation must adjust; a succeeding one need not. Paradoxically, to have lived longer is to have experienced more acutely our incapacity to come to terms with life in

the framework of the categories to which we have become accustomed; and the result is schizophrenic.

On the surface the changes we are witnessing can appear as
simply extraordinary and unmitigated progress. Man's capacities,
after all, are steadily increasing, and no limit to that increase is
clearly in sight. With the elaboration of more and more intricate,
more and more refined, instruments, man's capacity for perception has been extended enormously. In a period of twenty years
scientific knowledge has progressed both quantitatively and qual-
itatively more than it did in the centuries between Archimedes
and Einstein. Keeping pace with this growth in man's knowing
is the equally extraordinary increase in his know-how, in his
productive capacity to fulfill his needs (this last, of course, accompanied by a vast increase in those needs). Both these advances might simply be included under the heading of an
increased capacity to dominate nature—unfortunately most dra-
matically exemplified in the capacity for destruction, but also experienced as a capacity for construction. The forces of nature
have been harnessed for good as well as for evil.

THE NEED OF CRITERIA FOR CHANGE

When we witness the unquestionable increase in man's power
over his environment, however, we cannot but wonder whether
this increase is not inseparable from a diminishment in man's capacity to know himself, to control himself, to be creative of a
life suitable for man as man. With the enormous growth in his
capacity to know and do, there remains the gnawing question
whether man himself has grown. Along with growth in man's
capacities goes a multiplication of the problems which he must
face in his changing world, and we must at least ask the question
whether he has proved himself adequate to the task of facing
them. It would certainly be incredibly naïve to think that
change, just because it is change, is necessarily healthy change.
But has contemporary man increased his capacity for distinguishing between healthy and unhealthy change; has he perhaps re-
linquished any criterion for making that distinction? In a world
which is characterized by rapid change, by constantly accelerated change, it might be questioned whether man has retained a
capacity to give meaning to the term "should," to say what

should or should not be, or whether he has simply surrendered to what is or is in the process of coming to be. In an age far less externally complex than our own, Plato in his *Sophist* asked searching questions about the being of becoming, and the questions are no less in need of answers today than they were then. It may be that we see more clearly today that if philosophy is an attempt to grasp ultimate reality, and if ultimate reality is in process, then philosophy must come to terms with process. To know that this is so, however, is not to have solved the problem; it is not even to have attempted to understand the problem. If there is a *being* of process, then, it would seem, there should also be a *logic* of process. But what can this logic be? Can there be a static logic of dynamic process, or must the logic itself be dynamic? What can a dynamic logic be; can it be arrived at by an analysis of concepts, or must it somehow emerge from the process itself? Can an analysis of concepts ever do justice to the process from which they emerge? Whether or not definitive answers can be given to questions such as these, they make it clear that the issues involved are too problematic simply to be passed over in silence.

At one extreme, then, in relation to change is the attitude which either sees change as simply a fact which need not be judged in the light of any criterion whatever or accepts change as good merely because it is change. The problem generated by this extreme attitude is rather obvious: the attitude is not merely uncritical and, therefore, irresponsible; it is a relinquishing of the genuinely human role of determining what one is to be. It is the sort of attitude which, in recent years, has permitted B. F. Skinner to get such mileage out of his theories of human manipulation. At the opposite extreme is the attitude of a resistance to change because it violates an established order which itself has become the criterion for what is as it should be. The problem here is a subjective one (although the response to it may have objective overtones): the problem of identifying with one period in a world which is in fact changing. One who thus identifies the past with what is in the process of becoming can quite readily assign to himself the vocation of reversing change—to bring it into conformity with the arbitrarily accepted criterion—thus romanticizing the past, without reflecting that the past in question represents a change over a more remote past (the accelerated pace of change of which we have spoken can render this problem more acute without making the simplistic solution to it more valid). At no stage in history can it make sense to insist that only methods from the past are adequate to solve questions of the present or, worse still, that problems of the present must be adapted to solutions of the past. Here, too, the problem can be made more complex by a failure to see just what is changing, the sign or the thing signified. Where sign and signified are identified, a commitment to what is signified can result in resistance to any change in the manner of signifying it. A solution can be found, perhaps, in a knowledge of the past which permits one to understand and cope with ongoing change in the light of past change—if this is not, in turn, complicated by the difficulty of understanding a past which exists only in the record of it or of knowing just what happens when a change takes place.

CHANGES IN PAST CIVILIZATIONS

To illustrate this on the grand scale and with broad strokes, we might look at a series of stages in civilization as we know it, each ushered in by a cataclysmic change, even though not with the rapidity to which we are now forced to become accustomed. The story of the ancient East (i.e., that part of the East whose history has directly influenced the West—Egypt, Mesopotamia, Babylonia, Persia) is necessarily somewhat foggy, but it represents a civilization which had little in common with the Greco–Roman civilization which succeeded it in our history. The disintegration of the Roman Empire was, in turn, a change which gradually resulted in another diametrically opposed civilization, that of the Holy Roman Empire and of the feudal structures within it. As a sort of extension of feudalism we can see the great monarchies of the West, whose gradual demise was ushered in (symbolically perhaps) by the French Revolution, and which were superseded by the constitutional nation-states of nineteenth-century Europe. When we reach this stage we are faced with another revolution which was chronologically concomitant with the rise of nation-states but the repercussions of which wrought a tremendous change in civilization—we call it the Industrial Revolution. This stage in Western civilization was succeeded by a sort of vacuum wherein industrialization continued, but a style of life was coming to an end. The cataclysmic dividing-line was World War I (World War II simply continued the process of disintegration). A new age has been ushered in, and its multiple changes are ours to cope with—we can call it the atomic age, the space age, or what-have-you. The point is that the mentality of a former age cannot cope with it, any more than the mentality of feudal Europe could cope with the Industrial Revolution.

To speak of changes such as these, of course, is to say nothing of the myriad other changes which have taken place in the course of history; it is not even to spell out the implications of these major revolutionary changes. It does, however, show to some extent what change can be: not merely differences in living resulting from advances in technical knowledge, skill, development of transportation and communication, growth of population, etc., but changes in mentality, in ways of seeing reality, in taste, in values—in short, in most of the things which make up the spiritual life of man. Quite obviously, too, the changes which take place are not immediately worldwide—until most recent times changes have never been worldwide—but they do belong to a steady process which ultimately makes the life of every man vastly different from one age to another.

To illustrate at this point with but one significant example: even granted that in the course of human history God does not change, there can be no question that man's view of God changes again and again. Even apart from revelation, there is a passage from a plurality of gods to the one God, from the God of nature to the anthropomorphic God, from the purely transcendent to the more immanent God, from the God who is power and might to the God who is spirit and love. The change is one in man's awareness, it is true, but precisely that is significant. The fact is that we simply do not continue to say exactly the same when we say "God"—whether in successive periods in our own individual lives or in the course of history—and the change is a fundamental change in us, a change not only in our way of seeing God but in our way of seeing ourselves and the world. And this is as it should be. It is one of the reasons why we can—and perhaps should—have an unchanging commitment to God accompanied by a changing response, without inconsistency. More than that, changes such as these can be—and perhaps should be —paradigmatic for the changes which come about wherever there is vitality. It is not merely that with the passage of time man sees himself *differently*; what he sees in seeing himself is *different*; a changing image of man means a changing man, and our problem is to discover how the philosopher comes to terms with that.

There are, however, two questions here, one regarding the fact of change, and the other the desirability of change; and the questions can be kept separate. When philosophy enters upon the scene it can concern itself with either or both; it can seek to evaluate changes which take place or perhaps the desirability of effecting change. When Aristotle, for example, recognized the experience of change as incontrovertible evidence for the fact of change, he sought to describe the structure of reality in such a way as to account for the fact (Parmenides and Zeno, on the other hand, opted for a structure of reality which reason seemed to demand, thus preferring to ignore the evidence of experience). Philosophy, then, neither initiates nor guides change; like the Owl of Minerva it takes flight at dusk to gaze on what has already taken place and to give an account of it. Its task, however, is not simply to watch; it must also seek to understand, to evaluate, perhaps even to predict and warn. If, with Marxism, it seeks not merely to understand but also to bring about change, it may well be doing something admirable, but in becoming thus admirable it has become something other than philosophy.

EFFECT OF CHANGE ON MAN

Now, the change with which we are here concerned is not simply physical change, which might conceivably be explained by a theory of potentiality and actuality and not evaluated at all. Our concern is the more profound and ultimate concern of all philosophical investigation, which is man—man in the process of becoming what he is not yet. We seek to understand man, and we recognize that throughout the process man is always identifiable as man. This requires that we be able to distinguish between what belongs to man substantially and what belongs only to his changing styles of life; but it also requires that we do not allow a seemingly once-and-for-all answer regarding the meaning of man to blind us to the progressive realization of what it is to be man. There is a delicate balance to be maintained here. We can, after all, still read Homer and Sophocles, Plato and Aristotle, or the Bible, and recognize that the man we meet there is the man we meet when we know ourselves or when we reflect on our contemporary civilization. At the same time we must recognize that there is a difference, a vast difference, and one which cannot be accounted for by the mere passage of time. We must recognize, too, that the process of man's becoming will not be understandable by reference to some "plan" in the mind of God, which, even if it were the case, would not be available to the mind of man. We must seek to understand what man is by examining what man does, without at the same time surrendering to the sort of humanism which claims that man is intelligible as man only if God is eliminated from the picture.

The ultimate point of reference for all philosophy, then, is man, and all that man knows is ultimately a contribution to his knowledge of himself. This does not mean that all philosophy is reducible to psychology (or anthropology)—that would be inadequate, even as a "philosophy of man"—but it does mean that all philosophy knows is significant only in reference to man. It is man who knows, who does the questioning, and every answer he attains tells him more about himself. One might conceivably be interested, with Husserl, in the "essence" of consciousness, or of life, or of reality, independently of whether it is man's consciousness, or man's life, or reality in relation to man; but it is doubtful that the results of such an interest could mean a great deal, or that one could really escape the ultimate reference to him who is interested. We may be interested in logic or epistemology, but only because they tell us of human thinking. Our concern may be metaphysics, but it tells us of being-for-man. Ethics, too, is a guide, not to action in general, but to human action. A philosophy of nature (as opposed to science) seeks to penetrate the "meaning" of nature—for man. Even a philosophy of God seeks a knowledge which is significant as determining man's relationship to God.

We can go further and say that any particular philosophy— distinguished from philosophy as the total process of philosophizing—is significant not so much for its "truth value" (although that need not be negligible) as for the light it throws on ongoing human experience. Philosophy asks the kind of questions which are ultimately unanswerable—at least in the sense that what answers there are are not ultimate; that is why it is *perennis*—and the questions are those which no other discipline is even competent to ask, much less answer. To take but the most obvious example: the question of life. We cannot simply take life for granted, not our own view of it nor the most commonly accepted view of it. We must ask questions about it, and the questions are significant, even where no definitive answer is forthcoming—the questioning itself reveals man to himself. Is life better than non-life? Is biological life a supreme value, such that it may not be sacrificed for any other value? Is life a value only for the one who lives it? Is human life superior to other forms of life? What does "superior" mean in the context? As scientist, artist, jurist, politician, businessman, athlete, a man can get his work done without asking these and a host of other questions which his science, art, law, politics, business, or sport, can neither ask nor answer. As man he cannot be satisfied not to ask the questions, even though the lack of definitive answers forces him to ask them over and over again. Here, perhaps, we can detect a purpose which the philosopher serves, precisely as philosopher; he does in a disciplined way what all men have a tendency to do but most men do not have the time to do.

MAN IN SOCIETY

All these questions are questions about man, even where the direct object of the question is not man himself. The meaning of what is, what happens, what is done, is to be found in man, because only man is a bearer of meaning. Man, however, is concretely intelligible, concretely meaningful, only as he concretely is—and that is in society. We have said that to be conscious of man as man is to be conscious of man in process, but consciousness of man in process is inseparable from consciousness of society in process—and that is history. History bears witness to repeated changes in man's mentality, his way of seeing reality, his taste, the values he lives by; but these changes are inseparable from the changes of social structure wherein man lives.

Much of what has been said up to this point can, it is true, sound strange to Aristotelian ears. In the Aristotelian tradition, although man is "essentially" social and political (and perhaps, therefore, historical), he is still only derivatively so. His social and political character flows from his "nature"—his life follows from and, therefore, is not constitutive of his nature (the priority of *esse* over *agere* is looked upon as not simply logical but in some sense ontological). In this view, which in reality is basically a metaphysical view antecedent to any concrete consideration of man, relation is simply subsequent to and, therefore, not constitutive of substance. Now, where man as "nature" is significant (i.e., considered abstractly), it may make sense to speak in this way; where, however, there is question of man in the concrete, as "person," it makes little sense. It is, in fact, a moot question whether it makes sense at all to speak of man as a being of nature; man is truly man only as a person, and man is a person only as related to other persons (the Trinitarian analogy is not accidental). This means, then, that man is authentically human only in the framework of society, with its multiple relations. By the same token the process whereby man becomes what he is (better, perhaps, *who* he is) is inseparable from the process whereby society becomes what it is, and both are inseparable from what man does.

To say this is not to say that the Aristotelian view of man is erroneous—except in the sense that any partial view is erroneous if it is taken as total. It is a commonplace that many men can look at the same thing and yet *see* something different. The biologist, the psychologist, the social scientist, the rhetorician, the advertising man, the philosopher, and the theologian—all look at man. What each one sees is different, and what each one sees can in some sense be true. Similarly, different philosophers can see man differently, and their views can be partially true.

We are not saying, then, that to speak of man in society, of man as effectively human, acting precisely as concrete man and not as an abstraction, of man as intelligible only in a social framework, is to say all that can be said of man. The abstract foundation of human "nature" may well be necessary, if all else we say is to be intelligible. We are saying, however, that not to speak of man in society is not to speak of man as he is; it is to look at the evidence available and not to read all of it. When the individual enters the world, he enters a world which is not only already there but which already has a sense (the term signifies both "meaning" and "direction") which he does not give it and which he is not free to take away from it. He chooses neither to be born nor to be born in these circumstances. The society in which he lives has been structured by a sum of human activity and environmental forces in the past in which neither he nor those around him have had any part. It is a society which can, it is true, also be restructured, but even the restructuring will be socially conditioned. He will speak a language which he as an individual does not choose, a language which is a given in the community and which will condition the way he experiences the world and life in it. He will neither create nor discover values independently of others; his very thinking will be conditioned by the structured community of which he is part. The world of values in which he shares does not flow from nature—not even from "human nature"—although it may be "natural" for him to accept a certain set of values. As time goes on he will, undoubtedly, change in many ways, but the changes will not be independent of changes taking place in the social framework. In short, he will inevitably be part of a vital social organism which follows the two basic laws of all organisms: that the whole is greater than the sum of its parts and that the whole is somehow present in each of its parts.

In the course of his life the individual will learn many abstract truths, but because the whole of that life will be conditioned by a social contact, he will also learn that those abstract truths are rarely adequate to the concrete situation where the action is. If he is not to perish in the vacuum of those abstractions, he must discover that a certain healthy relativism is in order—not that the abstract truths will ever become abstractly untrue, but that in being concretized they will not be quite the same truths. What is abstractly true can continue to be true and yet be found concretely (practically) to be untrue, because things do not happen in the abstract, and what does happen deviates, be it ever so slightly, from the abstract prescription of how it should happen. Plato was not wrong in looking for the definition of abstract justice, any more than Galileo was wrong in calculating the formula for the rate of acceleration of freely falling bodies, or Kant in formulating the categorical imperative, because Plato, Galileo, and Kant knew that rules valid for an ideal order are only approximately valid for the real order. Moreover, circumstances can change so much that what could have been concretely meaningful in one set of circumstances becomes meaningless in another.

What immediately comes to mind by way of dramatic illustration is the defense of war drawn from the enumeration of the conditions for a just war. One need not deny the validity of the conditions nor the justice of the war they describe in order to be convinced that we have reached a point in history where the conditions cannot be concretely realized and where, as a consequence, "just war" has become a meaningless abstraction. We can, of course, speak in the abstract of intelligence, of beauty, of right, and we can know what we mean when we do. But we can also make the mistake of thinking of intelligence as the capacity for abstract conceptualization which is verified in IQ tests, or of beauty as the form which has been concretized in the art of a particular era, or of a right as the sort of claim a person has to a thing (e.g., to private property) within the framework of social relationships which are no longer existent. If we do this we run the risk of not recognizing intelligence, or beauty, or right, when they appear in forms or contexts to which we are not accustomed.

There is a tendency among philosophers to want what is true to be eternally true; it is more comfortable that way. If, of course, philosophers are content with abstractions, they may very well get what they want, but they may thus prove rather unreliable guides through life. We can, for example, speak of "inalienable rights," which, presumably, flow from nature and are not dependent on the relationships of society. The fact that at some time in history every one of those "rights" has been contravened by one society or another, or that only relatively recently have any rights been recognized as belonging to man as man and not merely to some particular kind of man (e.g., a free man), does not contradict the fundamental inalienability of the rights in question. That the list is so short, however, might lead one to suspect that a more fruitful approach to the question of rights might be through the social and political structures where rights become effective. Kant set down as an eternal, necessary, and universal truth that a human being is never to be treated as a means but only as an end. By this Kant certainly meant that human beings do not evolve in society to a point where such a categorical imperative becomes true (if, indeed, Kant was even capable of thinking of man as evolving). It may be that Kant was correct; but we should remember that the Kant who thought so was the same Kant who thought that physical laws were not merely descriptive of what does happen but rather prescriptive of what must happen, and who saw both physical and moral laws as prescribed by reason alone. It may very well be that inalienable rights are truly inalienable, but need the source of this inalienability be "nature" and not a set of relationships which have developed with the evolution of man's social consciousness?

THE DYNAMICS OF SOCIETY

Nothing which has been said so far should be taken as a claim that all other forms of explanation—in the physical, psychological, epistemological, metaphysical, or moral orders—should be dropped and replaced by sociopolitical or historical explanations (although it may well be that man's awareness of any and all explanations is conditioned by the social context within which he seeks explanations). It claims no more than that the philosopher should take the social into account in all his investigations. This is particularly true where what the philosopher is investigating are changes in human consciousness, changes in man's image of himself, of the world, and of God. Here it is important to stress that the social context, the social structures, of which we have been speaking are not static but dynamic. To investigate social or political changes themselves is, of course, the work of the sociologist or political scientist, but to investigate the impact of these changes on man, on the way man changes, or on the way his image of himself changes, is the work of the philosopher. Nor need this mean that the philosopher has made unnecessary concessions to the Marxist by interpreting all change exclusively in terms of the relationships which develop in the productive process (although these, too, should not be ignored—a theory need not be totally true in order to make important contributions to social understanding).

It does mean, however, a considerable reduction in the importance of studying man's "nature"—except to the extent that both his social being and the development of his consciousness through action and interaction reveal the need of a constant core of intelligibility which is indispensable—if process itself is to be intelligible. Only if that which evolves in the process is always identifiable as man and not as something else can talk of change in man's consciousness make sense. In fact, history can make sense only if it is constantly of man that it is the history. We can speak of a process of evolution whereby man comes to be man, but we cannot meaningfully speak of a history prior to the advent of man. By the same token, however, once man has evolved to the point of having become a social being, his development thereafter is inseparable from the development of the social structures within which he lives, acts, and interacts. So true is this that effectively the history of man and the history of society simply coincide. To speak with Teilhard de Chardin, we might say that social evolution is the form which evolution takes, once biological evolution has made of man a social being. Thus, his oft-quoted dictum that "the history of cosmogenesis is the history of anthropogenesis" can be expanded by saying that the history of anthropogenesis has become the history of sociogenesis —that is what the process of "complexity-consciousness" has become.

It is not without significance that philosophy as we know it, or history as we know it, or, for that matter, human awareness as we know it, began when man began to be aware of his social dimensions. A simple answer to this could be that man experienced no need to reflect on the meaning of reality, or of process, or of human awareness as such, until he experienced what it is to be with others with whom he felt a need to communicate. This is, after all, in its own way correct; the need of reflection on the meaning of existence is inseparable from the need of communicating one's reflections, no matter how solipsistic the "existentialist" may appear to want to be. Human thought thrives almost exclusively on the need and the desire to communicate itself. Communication, however, is meaningless unless there is a community within which communication can be accomplished. Man asks himself many questions, but the very asking of them would be devoid of meaning were there no community within which the questions could be asked. The individual cannot simply ask himself questions: unless the questions are asked against the background of a society which gives meaning to the individual, the individual cannot ask questions which make sense

—to say nothing of the impossibility of supplying answers. What it comes down to is that, although man can conceivably ask questions about man as man without reference to the social context in which man is found, he himself cannot be independent of the social context in asking such questions. Actually it is inconceivable that man in isolation (if there can be such) could even ask himself what it means to be man; the question could not occur to him outside a framework in which it is significant that others, too, should be men. So far as we know, dogs and cows, and cats and snails, do not ask themselves what it is to be what they are— not simply because they lack the intelligence to ask such profound questions, but because they lack the social framework within which alone such questions could possibly make sense. The result, then, is that the question regarding the meaning of man can be asked only in a framework within which the relationship of man to man is constitutive of the answer which can be given to the question. If this is so, however, then the answer to the question regarding the meaning of man is not to be found in abstract speculations concerning his "essence" or "nature," but in a concrete inquiry into the social structures which condition his life as he lives it. We can know neither what man is nor what he should be independently of the concrete relationships within which "is" is significant. We do not know man adequately, we might say, by simply knowing what he is or even what he does; we must also know how he relates.

This, however, brings us back once more to the problem (or the dilemma) of constancy. Change can be meaningful only if it is change in that which remains constant; constancy can be meaningful only if it is constancy enduring through change. The dilemma, of course, is not a new one for human thought; nor is it limited to the constancy and changeableness of man himself. The dilemma is as old as philosophy itself; it might even be considered as the greatest single impetus to philosophizing. To deny change (as, presumably, did Parmenides and Zeno) is to fly in the face of experience which is not to be rationalized out of existence. To deny constancy would be to condemn experience to meaninglessness. It may be that with Hume we will want to say that there is no way of "knowing" that what we experience retains a continuing identity with itself, that there is no "logical" contradiction in its being repeatedly annihilated and re-created. We do know, however, that we cannot *live* without supposing its continuing identity. If experience is to be the experience *of* anything, there must be constancy.

Thus, to say, as we have said, that man (or perhaps simply the image of man) changes, as social structures come to be and pass away, is to say that what is constantly identifiable as man has undergone significant development in a process we call history. The man of the Bible, of Sophocles and Plato, of Dante and Thomas Aquinas, of Hobbes and Rousseau, Hegel and Marx, Whitehead and Dewey, is the man we meet today when we experience ourselves or those who with us make up contemporary society. Nor is this necessarily to speak in any but an abstract sense of an enduring "nature" of man. There is, in fact, a danger that we shall look upon man as an eternally given, who may have his ups and downs but who can always be judged by the same standards, because he is an unchanging instantiation of an idea in the mind of God. To be changeless in this sense is to be a thing, not a person, and the most significant thing which can be said of any man is that he is a person, unique in the class to which he belongs. It may, of course, be that the requisite constancy of man also demands that certain characteristics, such as rationality or immortality, must always be true of him (although what we *mean* by these may also change), but this in no way requires that many of the things we say of him with utmost confidence need be true of him at every period in his history. To distinguish what we must always say of him (and the manner in which we say it) from what we must say of him in certain temporal and social circumstances is one of the tasks which confront the philosopher. There are questions which must always be asked with a realization that the same answers are not always valid, or at least that the answers do not retain exactly the same meaning.

CHANGES IN MAN'S VIEWPOINT

With Plato we can, for example, ask such questions as "What is justice?" The likelihood is that, along with Plato, we shall never find a completely satisfactory answer to the question, even though, if in formulating the question we come up with something like the *Republic*, we shall have done a very worthwhile thing. We are more likely, however, to ask what the just thing to do in a given set of circumstances is, or when a situation is just or unjust (with an effort, of course, to ensure that the *terms* "just" and "unjust" retain a constant *meaning*). It is when we ask this second sort of question that we must take into account all the circumstances which can vary the situation and, thus, the answer to the question. No one doubts that a knowledge of the circumstances is tremendously significant in arriving at this sort of judgment—that is one reason why a "categorical imperative" has such reduced practical value. It is important to note, however, that the structure of society in which events take place and choices are made is one of the most important circumstances to be taken into account, and that the structure of society can and does change with the advance of history. Perhaps what could correctly be called just or unjust in one form of society (e.g., a monistic one) cannot be so readily judged in another (e.g., pluralistic) form of society. We have already considered how questions regarding war or private property have to be asked differently within the framework of contemporary world society. There are other questions which have to be asked (and perhaps answered) differently against the background of changing relationships.

In any event, we should not take it for granted that an answer which could legitimately be considered adequate for a given social framework continues to be adequate when the framework has changed. It may be—to take a somewhat specialized example—that within the society for which the law was promulgated the indissolubility of marriage was unquestionable. It may be, too, that where the marriage union exactly reproduces the union there spoken of, its indissolubility is today equally unquestionable. But is the union exactly the same? Does the view which society takes of the union have some influence on the very "nature" of the union? Where the view that the "dynamics" of the union require a second look at its alleged permanency is socially so widespread, are we justified in ignoring it in favor of a view based on an abstract analysis of the "nature" of marriage? We might illustrate the nature of the question being asked by referring to what is today a dead issue (in the West at least), that of polygamy. There was a time when polygamy was quite normal, even among the chosen people of God. We may find it convenient to see this as a case of God's "permitting" what in itself was really evil; but, to say the least, that is a singularly unphilosophical (perhaps even blasphemous) convenience. We might also prefer to say that where society looked upon women (and women looked upon themselves) as possessions and, therefore—at least in this relationship—not as persons, it was perfectly logical not to consider the marriage union (or, perhaps, the procreative society) as an exclusive union of two equal partners. Or we might even prefer to say that the structure of early society did not make it imperative that there be one wife to a husband, whereas in contemporary society it is imperative. (What the situation may be in future society is a question we can mercifully leave unasked.)

Considerations such as these can permit us to approach other questions too. The arguments against birth control, for example, do not necessarily become bad arguments because the vast majority of people ignore them (although the *maior et sanior pars* argument might make moralists more humble). They might, however, become inapplicable arguments, where it is recognized that the marriage union is not primarily a procreative union and that intercourse is not merely a procreative act, or where overpopulation of the world is seen as a concrete problem, for which abstinence is too drastic a solution. We all recognize, of course, that the question of abortion cannot be solved by an appeal to the same considerations as those which apply to birth control. Nevertheless, without even going into the morality of abortion, we can ask ourselves whether it is always a good thing for morality to be legislated—particularly in a pluralistic society where the consciences of vast numbers of people differ so sharply. We are not likely to think that all the things which Plato legislated for in his *Laws* should be legislated for today. Perhaps we are ready to recognize that the legislation of morality in general should decrease—without, of course, denying that the "common good" is still a valid goal of legislation, *if* there are those who are truly wise enough to know what the common good is.

Perhaps we have even reached a point in history where we do not have to condemn out of hand those who argue that a law recognized as just can sometimes be justly disobeyed. I do not wish here to enter into the arguments for "civil disobedience," but I should like to suggest that an examination of them will reveal that they are not idiotic. In any event it would seem not inconceivable that the consideration of man as a member of society structured in a certain way can demand or permit what a consideration of man's abstract nature (or of society's "nature" in the abstract) does not.

It may be that there is an absolute morality which does not change with a change in social relationships, but it may be, too, that we have been wrong about the extent of such an absolute morality. It scarcely seems necessary to stress that there are existential moral demands which are no less binding because they did not aways bind; moral necessity is not a function of either eternal or universal validity. It might, of course, be said that fundamental moral principles remain always the same, and that change is only in that to which they are applied; but that is only another way of saying that the abstract remains always the same, while the concrete is process. This leaves intact the need of distinguishing between the abstract and the concrete. One can say, for example, that incest is always morally reprehensible, and that the application of this prohibition differs in different societies. Since, however, there is scarcely any form of what one society considers to be incest which is not permitted in some other society, the suspicion is that the relevant abstraction is not incest at all but something even more vague called "social desirability," which is meaningless except in the concrete context of the society where it is interpreted.

One of the reasons why laws change is that the social desirability of their implementation changes. There are a number of reasons why it is socially undesirable that fathers and daughters, mothers and sons, or even sisters and brothers, should marry. There was a time, in the era of the "extended family," when it was socially undesirable that third cousins should marry. We know, however, that Thomas Aquinas and the Scholastics sought reasons rooted in the abstract nature of love or in the rather tenuous ties of "blood" to explain *a priori* what was in fact a purely practical prohibition. Presumably there was a period in history (or there are social structures in existence) in which the marriage of brothers with sisters was (is) a practical social necessity. Whether there are biological reasons for frowning on such a practice is another question and one whose moral repercussions are quite different (here the biologist must speak before the philosopher can).

The point is that there are a great many givens in any society (and in history) which have long been considered to belong to the nature of things but which turn out to be social conventions and quite justifiable as such. The family, we are told, is a "natural" society, and so, for the sake of argument, let it be (although certain experiments in Israel might cast doubt even on that). Where there is a society, there should be some form of authority, and so, tradition tells us, the father is the "natural" head of the family, just as the husband is the "natural" head of the wife. The difficulty with this is that there are societies in which the mother is the head of the family, and it would be rather arbitrary on the part of Western moralists to say that this is "unnatural" or wrong. Even in our own society it is becoming increasingly evident that to speak of the husband as "head" of the wife is nonsense, and to call either father or mother, rather than both, "head" of the family is unrealistic. Involved in all this, of course, is the even larger issue of the dialectical character of authority, which makes it doubtful whether authority "resides" in anyone rather than simply being exercised by one rather than many.

It has always been recognized by moralists that certain rights and obligations are necessarily vague and unspecified, and that they are made specific by legislation in society. Thus, in human life there is a time when one passes from the relative irresponsibility of childhood to the beginnings of responsibility in adulthood, and this seems to be tied up with the capacity to reason adequately. Different societies (even different segments of one and the same society), however, determine that age differently; they even determine (rather arbitrarily) a different age for different responsibilities. Thus, there is a voting age, a draft age, a driving age, a drinking age, an age when people can marry without parental consent, etc. Sometimes there are objections to the arbitrariness of such specifications, particularly when they seem to contradict each other, but it is generally acknowledged that they are specifications which society is competent to make. The question arises whether society does not specify a great deal more in the area of rights and obligations, without resorting to legislation but simply by the way it is structured. It is as though, with the passage of time and the change in relationships brought about by myriad factors not consciously brought to bear on its development, society gradually recognizes the anomaly of certain things which it formerly took for granted. Perhaps, too, they become anomalies as circumstances change.

In any event, the impression can be created that new rights are being developed, when what is happening is that former ways of doing things are becoming incongruous in the light of the image of man which develops with society itself. Thus, for example, new aspects of the right of personal privacy develop, and such things as reading the letters of others—whether it be parents who read letters written by or to their children, or government officials who censor the letters of citizens—become unacceptable. What is happening, of course, is that the very thinking in regard to the relationship between authority and subjection to authority is being revamped and privacy takes on a new meaning. By the same token we are witnessing a change in attitude which no longer takes it for granted that the police may at their own discretion employ wiretapping or lie detectors in their efforts to combat crime. Perhaps, of course, authority—parents, government, the police—never had these rights, and we are just finding it out. But perhaps, too, the image of man which develops in a modern social context is what makes the formerly acceptable now incongruous. There was a time, after all, not only when authorities could act rather arbitrarily toward their subjects, but when it would not occur even to the subjects to question their right to do so.

Something similar has happened with respect to the ideas we now hold regarding the bodily integrity of the person. Although philosophers, it is true, have had many eloquent things to say (not all of them terribly convincing today) about the inadmissibility of bodily mutilation, that in itself came at a relatively late date in human history. Nor were the same philosophers quite so sensitive as we are today regarding torture or corporal punishment, short of mutilation. There still are, of course, such things as "police brutality" and "revolutionary terrorism," but by and large such tactics are repudiated by society (with significant abstentions on the part of those who advocate violence as a means to the righting of wrongs). More significantly, the whole question of punishment (particularly capital punishment) has come in for serious rethinking.

What all this comes down to is that we not only apply principles to fundamentally different situations and thus come up with answers which could well have been unintelligible in another age or another situation, but that we give different meanings to the terms we use in describing man's condition. The most obvious example of such a term which takes on different meanings in different forms of society—whether the differences be historical or ideological—is the term "freedom." I do not know whether the term, or even the concept, existed in the ancient kingdoms of the East, but it certainly existed with limited applicability in Greece and Rome. With the advent of Christianity, however, the term took on new meaning, because it was used to characterize the child of God as such. Strangely enough, even in Christianity, the term "free" became bogged down as a qualifier of *arbitrium*, and effective freedom was still long in being realized. Ever since then the term has had its ups and downs. In feudal times it did not say a great deal, and with the advent of capitalism it became something to characterize business enterprise or trade (i.e., the freedom of some to exploit others for the advantage of the former). All in all, however, despite advances and regressions, the term "freedom" seems to have taken on more concrete meaning, even though there may still be some doubt whether people know what they want when they want freedom. This is made all the more manifest when, in the same historical period, the notion of freedom can be ideologically so different. It is difficult to know whether the term means the same when used by an American capitalist, a Russian Communist, or a member of the "Third World." Nor is the difference merely one of different philosophies; the meaning of the term is conditioned by the social framework within which it is used and within which the freedom in question is to be exercised.

To confine ourselves to the social context with which we are familiar, we can say that significant changes have taken place, if not in the meaning of the term "freedom," at least in our conception of what we are free to do or not to do. It is recognized, for example, that the freedom associated with private enterprise can and should be severely limited by public responsibility. The industrialist is simply not free to dispose of what he owns if in doing so he will affect adversely the lives of thousands of workers. Little by little we have come to recognize that it is a function of government to regulate free competition, to limit the freedom of producers, to control those industries whose public impact is greatest. Although our society still recognizes in principle the private ownership of the means of production, it no longer accords absolute dominion over that private property. We see more and more clearly that what one does with one's private property can have an effect on the public domain (e.g., through pollution), and so we stress the necessity of control.

For a long time it was assumed that a wage contract was one entered into by two parties, an employer and an employee. Strangely enough, with the introduction of multiple (private) ownership of the means of production, the assumption remained that management still constituted one party to the contract, while the individual employee (worker) was the other. With the growth in size and wealth of the industrial enterprise, however, it becomes quite obvious that equality of rights between employer and employee is actually the grossest inequality; there is an extraordinary disproportion in bargaining power. The development of labor unions evened the balance somewhat; but even with the increased bargaining power for the employee thus brought about, the need for some sort of government supervision and control becomes rather obvious. The result is that social changes have brought about a change in our thinking so that we now simply take for granted both collective bargaining and a measure of government control, not as obstacles to freedom but as guarantees of equal freedom.

In a somewhat more subtle way the notion of "social justice" —a relatively new concept for the philosopher—provides an additional set of checks and balances for freedom. To a great extent it has become illegal to discriminate against human beings on grounds of race, creed, color, national origin, and even sex. Gradually it is becoming clear that it can even be immoral to discriminate in cases where it is not yet illegal. It can be immoral to exercise one's "freedom of choice" in choosing one's companions on such a basis (e.g., in private schools or clubs). One could, of course, argue that it always was immoral, and that we are just beginning to realize it. The fact is, nevertheless, that a relatively extensive change in thinking has taken place, and that the social change has preceded and influenced the change in thinking. It seems, therefore, necessary to say that what is justifiable exercise of freedom in one age or social context can become unjustifiable in another. If we add to this that world-society has become a reality in a way it never was before, it may become necessary to redefine the relationship of man to man as such.

Although it would be out of place here to introduce even the terminological opposition of "conservatism" and "liberalism," since the very meaning of the terms varies so greatly, it does seem necessary to ask whether there is not a certain self-defeating factor in the kind of conservatism which resists change on principle. When, as we noted before, the attempt is made to adapt methods of the past to problems of the present, one wonders whether in reality the attempt is to adapt the problems of the present to the methods of the past. This brings up the question of the need for rethinking many of our categories, not in order to get rid of them, but in order to test their validity in circumstances out of which they did not emerge. This, of course, can work in two directions: it should prevent us from seeking to understand present situations in the light of inapplicable past categories; but it should also keep us from judging past situations in the light of categories which have emerged more recently in the process of history. It is too obvious to need mentioning that there have been many changes of thinking in the course of time, but it still needs to be asked whether to these changes in thinking there correspond real changes in man; changes in social attitudes, it would seem, are attended by concrete changes in personality. If the image of man changes from age to age or from social context to social context, is there not some real sense in which man changes?

It is all very well to say categorically that no man can own another man. Effectively there was a time in history when men did own other men, precisely because the image of man which was then current did not make such ownership abhorrent. Was, for example, the fact of slavery in the early United States an evil simply because it was slavery, or because the Western image of man had advanced to the point where slavery had become an anachronism? We have little doubt today that the kind of serfdom which was common in the Middle Ages is simply intolerable. Can we honestly say that we know now that it was intolerable then? Most of us have little difficulty in accepting today's wage contract as justifiable at least in principle. May the situation not change to the point where the wage contract will be as unacceptable as serfdom? It may, of course, be argued that what is or is not acceptable along these lines will depend on legislation. Strictly speaking, however, the legislation becomes an effective possibility only when a way of thinking changes, and a way of thinking changes only when a set of relationships has already changed. There are other changes which we may be slow to accept, but they are with us to stay—at least for a while—and we shall have to adapt our thinking to them. We can, of course, delay the process by, for example, concocting funny stories about "the organization man"; but one day we are going to have to admit that man has become just that, and we are going to have to adjust our thinking to it. What will our thinking be if in the foreseeable future two per cent of the world's population becomes capable of supplying the material needs of the whole population? It seems clear that the categories for handling such a situation are not yet available.

Perhaps here is where the contemporary difficulty lies. The past has seen changes as cataclysmic as any we witness today. They did not occur, however, with the same rapidity, and men had more time to adapt their thinking—imperceptibly—to the changes. Today changes outrun thought, at least the thought whereby man thinks what it is to be man—and so, the crisis. Perhaps we can weather the crisis only if we adopt an attitude which is illustrated in Nietzsche's image of life. Life, he tells us, is like a pathway which exists only as we walk it. Behind us it is constantly being rolled up, so that we can really not look back and find our direction there. In front of us it unfolds only with each forward step we take. Where the path leads, then, is not antecedently given, and yet the direction it takes is not arbitrary or fortuitous. Only with great courage can we take the risk of walking down that path; but if we do not take the risk, we go nowhere.

voke certain features of a situation, citing differences in regard to race, creed, color, etc., which serve as morally relevant features to support his nationalism. In reality, the phenomena of nationalism are fairly easy to dispel logically—albeit not so, psychologically. Hare recommends simply asking the nationalist n who opposes nation N whether n would think it right to perform an act of aggression against N if he, n, were a citizen of N and, like other *de facto* members of N, did not wish to be attacked by n and his nationalistic colleagues. As a result of such a Kantian query, most nationalists will soon realize the illogic of their demands and relent against N, thereby revealing the prudential, egotistical nature of their original pseudo-moral dictate. The strategy on Hare's part has been to point out the conceptual implications of "right": namely, that no two actions can differ in regard to rightness (or wrongness) *solo numero*. Given Hare's argument, a sincere but pure nationalist would be left holding an untenable view since he would have failed to satisfy the formal requirement of universalizability.

To remain immune to Hare's counter, the nationalist must retreat to fanaticism. Moreover, a fanatical form of nationalism—that is, a commitment to a set of ideals which passes the test of prescriptive universalizability—can, for Hare, be immune to logical attack. The real fanatic may be prepared to sacrifice, not only all the interests of others, but his own as well, out of a zeal fostered by his ideal! Yet Hare foresees little cause for pessimism herein, since the true fanatic is a "very rare bird indeed."

To appreciate better Hare's logical apparatus as a tool of peaceful negotiation, suppose we consider the case of a nationalist (of a socialistic bent) who subscribes to a policy of collectivization of agriculture, and is prepared to wage war against any nation preventing the implementation of such a policy. Is there herein any hope for peaceful reconciliation? I believe Hare would answer "yes" on at least two counts. First of all, he would say, one might by empirical evidence rationally convince such a nationalist that his policy of collectivization actually stifles food production and severely handicaps the living standards of his country's farmers. But should our nationalist not falter, then, Hare would suggest, one might ask him to project himself phenomenologically into the situation of his antagonists (i.e., to put himself on the receiving end) and to ask himself if he would want to be attacked if he did not subscribe to such an agrarian policy. Implementing Hare's second suggestion would have the effect of exposing the nationalist's prudentialism, and since he had failed to pass the test of universalizability, the nationalist would forfeit his previous plea of moral righteousness. (It should be noted that Hare's test of universalizability could apply even if our agrarian reformer's policy should be determined by the empirical data to be the most economically feasible.)

Should the nationalist disregard the above two moves and retreat into fanaticism, then the aims of peace break down. The non-fanatical nationalist in contemplating such moves recognizes himself as his own worst enemy, and accordingly refuses to adopt such a logical maneuver. Hare seems to suggest that the non-nationalistic fanatic is powerless for want of sufficient supporters. But the serious threat to world peace remains in the person of the nationalistic fanatic. Yet Hare is optimistic, for

> if all nations were composed of very clear-headed, well-balanced people, in secure circumstances, with full access to the facts through a free and undistorted press, and if, with the aid of philosophers and others, they thought hard and continuously about their nation's policies, and in the end decided on them by majority vote, then there would be no danger at all of fanatical policies getting adopted.[3]

To recapitulate: Hare foresees three ideological barriers to peace —nationalism, non-nationalistic fanaticism, and nationalistic fanaticism. Given the right sort of philosophical spadework, Hare believes that these three obstacles can be surmounted.

Paradoxically, Hare's universal prescriptivism suggests that we all be fanatics on one score: that is, fanatics for peace who "attempt to do our best for the interests of all, with impartiality, i.e., justice, between persons."[4]

Although there is much to commend about Hare's program for peace, a few critical remarks seem nonetheless in order. First of all, one should be quite hesitant about admitting a "breakdown" in moral reasoning in the case of the fanatic, be he of a nationalistic bent or not. Peace is challenged, not by moral agents, but by non-moral fanatics who place themselves outside the boundaries of morality. Unlike Hare, then, I am reluctant to grant moral invincibility to the fanatic. One could attribute at most a perverse form of logical invincibility to such a person. Hence, emphasis by Hare on the *formal* characteristics of moral reasoning (i.e., prescriptivity and universalizability coupled with Hare's own version of expedient utilitarianism), no doubt historically an outgrowth of his acceptance of Hume's "is–ought" dichotomy (coupled with his own animus toward a meta-ethics of emotivism), need not blind us to the recognition of a fundamental content of human needs which demarcate the provenance of the moral. Philippa Foot puts the point well when she writes: "A man can no more decide for himself what is evidence for rightness and wrongness than he can decide what is evidence for monetary inflation or a tumour on the brain." [5]

Secondly, one gets the persistent impression that for Hare peace is merely an absence of war or a cessation of hostility. But surely a truce or an armistice (cf. Richard M. Nixon's "generation of peace" promise) does not secure a perpetual peace. Suppose that there were neither nationalists nor fanatics populating the political domain and that all men adopted the moral point of view. Would there then be peace? Perchance there would, but it would certainly not be guaranteed. Accordingly, Hare's concern centering on the externals of how to "make the peace" or "keep the peace" rather than on how to "be at peace" or "live in peace" obscures the more fundamental pursuit of peace which aims, not simply at removing certain logical difficulties preventing a condition of tranquil public order, but at restoring a personal sense of moral concord within the perimeter of community, a community of transcendental dimension. Doubtless, given the present world situation, we would all settle for the former, but if I am not mistaken, only the latter provides a lasting peace. What it means to "be at peace" or "live in peace," therefore, awaits philosophical elucidation.

Paradoxically, this more fundamental question may be altogether beyond man's purview. Perhaps he can only aspire to be a peacemaker in this life and never himself be at peace in this life. Should this prove an appropriate analysis of the human condition, I can suggest only that we find solace in the theistic adage: "Blessed are the peacemakers, for they shall be with Me in peace."

Indeed, it is my contention that a necessary condition for being in perpetual peace involves a commitment to live an agapeistic lifestyle, albeit the ontological force behind such a recommendation is no Braithwaitean "picture preference," but rather a transcendent God whose lifestyle, as presented in the historical personage of Christ, suggests a set of values to be imitated.[6] It will no doubt be suggested that I have plainly branded myself a theological voluntarist by such a move, and hence committed the Euthyphro-fallacy of judging a certain act x as obligatory because it is commanded by God, and not commanded by God because it is obligatory. To be sure, I do wish to espouse a form of religious morality (perhaps more aptly termed theistic descriptivism) to the extent that I believe the claims of religion and those of morality to be compatible with one another, albeit logically independent from one another; but I would deny that I thereby commit a "supernaturalistic fallacy" (i.e., by claiming that divine decrees logically entail what is morally obligatory or that basic ethical terms are defined in terms of the will of God).

To be sure, the compatibility referred to is decidedly not that described by W. W. Bartley in his recent book *Morality and Religion*.[7] Bartley claims that there is a unique union between the sphere of morality and that of religion. Invoking the Bloomsbury distinction between *one's religion* (i.e., a concern with one's psychological harmony and personal attitude toward the ultimate) and *one's morals* (i.e., directing the former to the practical realm), Bartley suggests that the bifurcation is only apparent, not real. To cope with the evil of the world, the remedy for conquest is to be sought in salvation, in Jungian wholeness, or in Socratic awareness, etc., with these inner states of awareness developing from and solidifying in our external behavior: "We are much at the mercy of our projections—that is, in the psychological sense, those interior states which we impose on the external world in the course of interpreting it."[8]

Yet when faced with a situation of possible conflict between one's religion and one's morals, Bartley sides with the former, which of course is not religion in the traditional, cognitive sense. Indeed, Bartley's admiration for the Bloomsbury circle is almost unchecked: "And in the course of their interior quests they did not preen themselves only on the pretty. . . . [T]hese persons transformed not only themselves and one another; in our century they transformed . . . ethics, economics, publishing. . . ." [9] It is surely a queer sort of theist who could take delight in J. M. Keynes' recollection of the Bloomsbury era: "Nothing mattered except states of mind, our own and other peoples', of course, but chiefly our own. These states of mind were not associated with action or achievement or with consequences. They consisted in timeless, passionate states of contemplation and communion. . . ." [10] Perhaps; but, morally speaking, Moore's *Principia Ethica* has never influenced the world, and what by comparison looked to Keynes like a handbook for politicians may, if what I have suggested is correct, just succeed.

Leaving aside the eccentric, prudential account of religious morality presented by Bartley, it seems to me logically possible for man to recognize the moral need of perpetual peace, but psychologically speaking difficult for him to implement this aspiration in practice. Hence the need of a model to serve both as the psychological lever to effect such a program of aspiration toward perpetual peace, and as the ontological lever to effect its concrete realization. Can an atheist or agnostic be a man of peace? Can a universe of godless nations effect the conditions of perpetual peace? Perhaps; but at best such a desideratum would be coincidental and would suggest obliquely some latent understanding of divine law. Moreover, since men and nations have never been at peace either with each other or with themselves, my suggestion is not that quixotic.

I take it that what is truly morally obligatory for man is what is most in accord with his fundamental needs, desires, and interests *qua homo sapiens*. But the beginning of wisdom is fear of the Lord, and the eternal law admonishes man to strive to be at peace with one another and with himself. I believe the following remark of Peter Geach's is appropriate, and in this case, at least, the sinner has received no "gratuitous mercy":

> It is reasonable to expect, if the world's whole raison d'être is to effect God's good pleasure, that the very natural agents and operations of the world should be such as to frustrate and enrage and torment those who set their wills against God's. If things are not at present like this, that is only a gratuitous mercy, on whose continuance the sinner has no reason to count.[11]

I now wish to adumbrate a metaphysical thesis to the effect that a state of perpetual peace can be attained only if moral agents carry out the practical exigencies of divine prescription such that a just God rewards them for their moral labors by granting them salvation in an afterlife, an afterlife which secures the conditions under which such a perpetual peace may be occasioned. Hence, the quest for peace is ultimately associated with the theistic belief in personal immortality. Accordingly, it becomes imperative, given such a thesis, to investigate the philosophical possibility of life after death by raising the Wittgensteinian question whether death is merely an event in life, or simply the end of life.[12]

Clearly, one's reason for maintaining a view that death is merely an event in life, and indeed one's whole psychological attitude toward the phenomenon of death, and the many conceptual puzzles surrounding the issue of an afterlife, are intimately related to one's basic position in regard to the relationship between mind and body. Accordingly, if the thesis of logical behaviorism were philosophically acceptable in holding that all psychological statements can be reduced to the physicalistic idiom, or if the thesis of identity were acceptable in holding that all psychological states are *de facto* identical with cerebral events, then, given such materialistic conceptual frameworks, one's entire attitude toward death and the possible logical offshoot of immortality would be greatly affected.

My own method of support for the view that death is merely an event in life and not the end of life is based on the indirect proof of criticizing the thesis of materialism, as well as excessive dualistic claims (that a person is just a disembodied entity), and thereby leaving open the possibility of there being a mental remnant (a discarnate personality) which persists at death. The form of dualism I am indirectly affirming is that the concept of a person's mind has a secondary role compared to the primary category of a human being to whom both states of consciousness and physiological predicates are attributed. This view, coupled with a rational belief in God,[13] allows for the possibility of there being an afterlife, so that one need not fear death as the destruction of the life process, or the negation of our aspirations for peace, albeit one may very well fear a post-mortem life under divine scrutiny.

I should caution that the development of a philosophical case for immortality need not be a comforting thought. It seems clear that a person might be genuinely bereaved by the possibility of his overcoming death. To such a person, immortality could be a bore (what counts is not the duration but the quality of post-mortem life) and/or a state of eternal misery (the philosophical correlate of hell). That is, I wish to agree with Dante that the afterlife holds both its rewards and its punishments so that the quality of life to be experienced in the hereafter very much depends on our ante-mortem moral character. H. H. Price writes: "The sort of world activity which a discarnate personality experiences after death corresponds to the habitual thoughts and wishes of that personality, including thoughts and wishes which were unconscious or repressed in earthly life." [14]

Today, identity theory and reductive materialism have greatly captured the allegiance of philosophers. Technically, the two positions are not strictly equivalent, because J. J. C. Smart, the principal proponent of identity theory, rejects Richard Rorty's[15] eliminative materialism: "I regard this as a retreat because it seems on the face of it implausible to relegate talk of our aches, pains, and the like to the realm of talk of witches and poltergeists. . . ." [16] Nonetheless, sophisticated philosophical differences aside, the materialist maintains that consciousness is identical with brain processes, just as genes are identical with DNA molecules, or heat identical with mean kinetic energy. To be sure, states of consciousness (i.e., sensations, volitions, thoughts, emotions, etc.) are intimately associated with brain states and the physico-chemical operations of the central nervous system. For instance, a prefrontal lobotomy drastically alters a man's personality; the use of sodium pentathol greatly slows down conscious episodes; and damage to the occipital cortex deters rational capabilities. But close association is not a relation of identity! Systematic correlation is not identity! To be sure, it remains futile to accuse the reductive materialist of maintaining an absurd position because, for example, "pain" does not have the same meaning as "stimulation of my C-fibers." The reductive materialist claims only a *de facto* (extensional) identity between brain states and psychological states, and would caution the non-materialist that Frege has warned us of the philosophical hazards of linking the extensional with the intentional realm. For example,

I may know the temperature of a certain body but be unaware of its mean molecular kinetic energy, but my knowing (or not knowing) does not confer an ontological distinction in nature. Reductive materialism cannot be so perfunctorily dismissed.

Nonetheless, I do believe there are some viable philosophical objections to reductive materialism. First of all, it might be argued that the alleged identity in question provides a mere causal explanation of the mental phenomena in question and not an analysis of their true nature. Norman Malcolm supports this point well when he writes:

> Not only cannot a brain *display* interest or anger, but it could not have *objects of interest* or *occasions for anger*. It could not engage in any of the activities that are required for the application of those concepts. A brain does not have the right physiognomy nor the capacity for participating in any of the forms of life that would be required for it to be a subject of experience.[17]

Secondly, the logic of intensional properties (we speak of persons as *hopeful, fearful, angry*, etc., and only metaphorically that way of cadavers or automata) differs from that of extensional properties. These properties seem to be ontologically irreducible to the extensional level. The identity theory seems then somewhat *ad hoc* in arguing that intensional properties are not genuine attributes of anything, but merely grammatical properties of something. George McGovern, for example, clearly had the real property of being *unpopular* with the American presidential electorate in 1972.

Moreover, the reductive materialist seems guilty of a category mistake of sorts. That is, certain extensional properties which apply to psychological states do not apply to physical states. For instance, a person's beliefs are said to be true, false, unsupported, eccentric; a person's after-images are said to be purple, green, yellow, etc.; but it is a linguistic howler similarly to attribute these properties to cerebral states. Rorty would reply that if we could psychologically condition ourselves to using neurological predicates to replace phenomenal predicates like *intense, throbbing*, etc., then our experience would be of entities which have such physiological properties. Rorty bases his view on the alleged truth of the "Myth of the Given" that there is no prelinguistic givenness about sensations which our language must report. I think C. J. Ducasse puts the non-materialist counter well, when he remarks:

> What thought, desire, sensation, and other mental states are like each of us can observe directly by introspection. . . . [T]hey do not in the least resemble muscular contraction or glandular secretion, or any other known bodily events. No tampering with language can alter the observable fact that thinking is one thing and muttering quite another; that the feeling called anger has no resemblance to the bodily behavior which usually goes with it; or that an act of will is not in the least like anything we find when we open the skull and examine the brain. Certain mental events are doubtless connected in some way with certain bodily events, but they are not those bodily events themselves. The connection is not identity.[18]

Accordingly, I would take issue with the thesis of reductive materialism which would allow us to drop our present discourse about psychological states in general, and replace it with neurophysiological discourse without loss of descriptive or explanatory power. James Cornman expresses the non-materialistic position well in remarking:

> Thus because "stimulation of C-fibres" taking on the descriptive role of "pain" accomplishes only the elimination of "pain" and not its role in true descriptions, such an elimination of sensation-terms fails to help the eliminative materialist. Indeed, if this is the only way sensation-terms can be eliminated, we should reject eliminative materialism, because we must either keep sensation-terms to make true descriptions or change physicalistic terms in such a way that using them descriptively implies that there are sensations.[19]

The reductive materialist, in summary, has attempted to present a case against the thesis that death is merely an event in life, and to suggest that as a matter of contingent fact materialism is true. I have attempted to argue that such a program is a failure. However, some linguistic analysts have presented an even stronger thesis: namely, that, given our linguistic structures, dualism and its logical offshoot, the survival hypothesis, is a meaningless thesis.

Antony Flew[20] has presented a poignant counter to the meaningfulness of the thesis of immortality. Flew claims that the expression "We all of us survive death" is self-contradictory, for the terms "death" and "survival" are mutually exclusive. Flew asks us to consider the possibility of a man's witnessing his own funeral: "For there is all the difference in the world between: imagining what it would be like to witness my own funeral (which requires only a minor effort); and imagining what it would be like to witness me witnessing *my own* funeral (which is logically impossible)."[21] In short, Flew argues that the concept of post-mortem experience (so essential to a philosophical elucidation of the thesis that death is merely an event in life) is meaningless, for there must be a subject of these experiences, and in death there can be no such subject. Cartesian talk is mere idle chatter; as inane as talk of a "faceless grin."

Nonetheless Flew's linguistic dismissal of the meaningfulness of death talk by reference to the non-empirical "magisterial neutrality" (Rorty's expression) of ordinary-language fails to provide the intended materialistic therapy. Indeed, even philosophers of a materialistic bent (e.g., Paul Edwards) have criticized the "unimaginability argument" of Flew *et al.* by contending that it confuses the content of a thought with the fact of its temporal occurrence in the life of a person. James Van Evra has recently argued that in no metaphysical sense have we an awareness of death viewed as the complete cessation of experience, but that it is nonetheless meaningful to employ the concept of death as a limit which acts as an ordering function to guide our lives. That is, much as the limit of the visual field is unseeable, so too death is unexperienceable; yet it is permissible to employ the concept of death while still admitting that there are no experienceless selves. "The significance of the limit is not as something independently real, but as an operational device."[22]

Herein Flew seems to be confessing somewhat obliquely his allegiance to a non-dualism of sorts, for he admits that person words do not refer to any incorporeal, ghost-like entity. Yet Flew seems to admit that a person may be more than his bodily parts, albeit whatever *more* there is perishes at death—that is, upon dissolution of the bodily organism. "Person words do not mean either bodies or souls nor yet any combination of the two. . . ."[23] This remark suggests to me intimations of immortality, for if Flew's thesis is intended to be more than a conceptual analysis of how we use person words, and is meant to encompass an ontological analysis as well, then surely persons are more than their physiological ingredients, and death *could* be an event in life, and the phrase "I survived death" not at all a linguistic howler. To be sure, Flew (like Freud) may be correct in saying that each one's death is unimaginable when conceived as the dissolution of his personhood, but not as the disintegration of his physical parts. One might compare on this score the recent medical findings of Dr. Nils-Olaf Jacobson, who, experimenting with terminal patients, placed their deathbeds on sensitive scales, and claimed that upon the advent of (medical) death, the corpses were found to weigh 21 grams less, thereby suggesting that the departed soul has some extensional property—in this case a weight of ¾ of an ounce! Such discoveries suggest that the survival hypothesis is both conceptually meaningful and empirically testable.

H. H. Price has countered Flew's "unintelligibility" thesis with the claim that one can provide a logical description of such post-mortem experiences: namely, the depiction of an image-world in which astral bodies are perceptible to one another via telepathic communication.[24] However, I am inclined to believe that the elaborate depiction by Price of such post-mortem person experiences raises more logical difficulties than it surmounts. One suspects that the psychological description involved is attenuated beyond logical recognition, and in spite of Price's disclaimers, his communities of disembodied existents seem isolated in a solipsistic paradise at best, inasmuch as the discarnate existent's life consists in acts of imagination and reflection in which each person has his *sui generis* internal processes as objects of awareness.

Price has very recently found a trace of a rapprochement between the so-called rival theories of embodied *versus* disembodied survival.[25] The former hypothesis speaks of an astral body belonging to a post-mortem personality which in turn occupies a quasi-material environment. The objects or post-mortem existents comprising this ethereal community are said to be endowed with both spatial (e.g., size, shape, location, etc.) and causal (e.g., weight, magnitude, resiliency, etc.) properties. By comparison, the disembodied personality occupies a dream-world which still need not be solipsistic, inasmuch as dream-images are spatial in some respects, albeit not located in physical space. Accordingly, there could be, even given this latter hypothesis, a public image-world which is the direct result of telepathic communication between disembodied personalities. The rapprochement between the accounts consists in noting the "family-resemblance" of the two accounts in that both hypotheses posit some sort of quasi-material, communal domain to avoid the charge of being purely spiritualistic. Price writes:

> For it seems that this "Next World" matter has what has been called an *ideoplastic* character. It is responsive, as it were, to the thoughts, memories and desires of the discarnate persons who perceive it, and the particular form it takes depends on the kind of person that one is.[26]

Despite the elaborate descriptive detail contained in Price's conceptual elaboration of a "Next World," and the wealth of parapsychological data used to give empirical support to such a survival hypothesis, I remain of the opinion that the only possibility of personal immortality consists in Divine Omnipotence's resurrecting our (corporeal) bodies. I thereby sympathize with Peter Geach's contemporary restatement of the traditional Thomistic view of interactionism and its inherent ramifications for a thesis of immortality.[27] Like Geach, I am inclined to dismiss Cartesian (and Pricean) talk of "ethereal bodies" because contemporary scientific canons give us little account, if any, of their mysterious activity; and I would question the meaningfulness of attributing at least some psychological states to disembodied existents, for I fail to understand how sensation-talk can be ontologically rooted to that which has no physical counterpart (e.g., how can there be sight without an optic nerve?). In short, I would tend to agree with Wittgenstein's suspicions of the privacy thesis of meaning, which engenders the Cartesian projects of Price, for surely we do not get the concept of "pain" by having a pain, any more than we get the concept of "minus quantity" by running up an overdraft. Yet, as a result of my previous criticism of reductive materialism coupled with a (Strawsonian) ontology of a fundamental distinction between mental and physical (predicates) states, I would entertain the Thomistic possibility of there being a mental remnant which persists upon bodily dissolution. I would, with Geach, attribute cognitive and volitional states to such a discarnate personality, but not, as would Price, sensations.[28] In short, Aquinas seemed correct in noting that *anima mea non est ego*, so that without the theistic hypothesis of corporeal resurrection there can be no hope of personal immortality, and assuredly no hope of attaining perpetual peace.

As a result of logical positivism's critique of religious language, many friends of religion attempt to develop often intricate noncognitive versions of theism, as it were, to establish the meaningfulness of religious claims within the conceptual framework of verificationism. One such recent effort in this direction is D. Z. Phillips' *Death and Immortality*.[29] Phillips finds survival after death just as meaningless an hypothesis as does Flew, yet unlike Flew claims nonetheless to believe in immortality! Disregarding the heuristic Pauline simile of a planted seed which grows into corn, Phillips agrees with Flew that "there is no such process which makes talk of buried corpses leading to new bodies rising from the dead intelligible to us."[30] In short, Phillips wishes to suggest that some form of post-mortem existence is not a necessary presupposition of belief in immortality, and at least indirectly to suggest that a state of perpetual peace is attainable in this world.

In committing himself to a linguistic framework in which meanings are associated with performances of certain language games in a shared way of life, Phillips proceeds to speak of "religious pictures" in which the believer shares in the life of God. This constitutes a form of immortality, but questions of truth and evidence are not applicable to such picture preferences, for they themselves ultimately prove the very measure of assessment. That is, questions about whether a man has an immortal soul or not are not empirical (i.e., not questions to which neurophysiology or parapsychology could determine an answer) but rather "questions about the kind of life he is living."[31] Phillips has in mind the notion of purification described in Plato's *Phaedo*, and by the Kierkegaard of *Purity of Heart* who speaks of eternal life as the reality of goodness in terms of which a person's life is assessed. "Eternity is not an extension of this present life, but a mode of judging it. Eternity is not *more* life, but this life seen under certain moral and religious modes of thought."[32] The purport of this non-cognitive interpretation of immortality is that dying to the self or self-renunciation wherein the believer participates in the life of God is the crux of immortality. Death, in brief, lies in alienation from God; immortality, in union with God.[33]

Indeed, Phillips suggests that the reality of God is simply a matter of one's intentional attitudes, therein conflating propositions *de re* with propositions *de dicto*. "In learning by contemplation, attention, renunciation, what forgiving, thinking, loving, etc. mean in these contexts, the believer is participating in the reality of God; *this is what we mean by God's reality*." [34] Ironically enough, given such an analysis of the immortality-thesis, it would seem senseless to continue to speak of "prayers of the dead" or any "activity of the dead," yet Phillips commits such howlers! [35] It may well be that the classical doctrine of survival after death rests on a mistake; to be sure, it is beset with conceptual difficulties. However, given Phillips' own analysis of the doctrine of immortality, it seems safer to apply Prichard's verdict to such an account.

To recapitulate: it has been my intention to show in this rather speculative essay how the thesis of immortality can be held to be both conceptually meaningful and empirically supportable. I suspect that one's attitude toward death is molded greatly by such a philosophical belief. Most assuredly, the quest for perpetual peace rests upon the veridicality of the survival hypothesis and the truth of theism. For some the belief in death as an event in life holds cause for hope and unrestrained joy. For others such a belief has the inverse effect of engendering fear and grief. I, for one, hope to be among the blessed and to attain the only real peace, "consisting as it does in the perfectly ordered and harmonious enjoyment of God and of one another in God." [36]

NOTES

1. Immanuel Kant, *Perpetual Peace*, ed. Lewis White Beck (Indianapolis: Bobbs-Merrill, 1957), p. 10.

2. R. M. Hare, *Applications of Moral Philosophy* (Berkeley: University of California Press, 1972), pp. 71-89.

3. *Ibid.*, p. 83. See Kant's *Perpetual Peace*, which attempted to frame a philosophical program directed at establishing a world government of federated nations under universal law.

4. Hare, *op. cit.*, p. 88.

5. Philippa Foot, "Moral Arguments," *The Definition of Morality*, edd. G. Wallace and A. D. M. Walker (London: Methuen, 1970), p. 177.

6. It is significant that R. B. Braithwaite's non-cognitive interpretation of religious language in *An Empiricist's View of the Nature of Religious Belief* (Cambridge: Cambridge University Press, 1955) omits the invoked passage of support in Paul's 1 Corinthians, Chapter 13, which states: "Love . . . delights in the *truth*."

7. W. W. Bartley, *Morality and Religion* (London: Macmillan, 1971).

8. *Ibid.*, p. 62.

9. *Ibid.*, p. 66.

10. J. M. Keynes, *Two Memoirs* (London: Hart-Davis, 1949), p. 83.

11. Peter Geach, *God and the Soul* (New York: Schocken, 1969), p. 129.

12. See Ludwig Wittgenstein, *Tractatus Logico-Philosophicus*, trans. D. F. Pears and B. F. McGuinness (New York: Humanities Press, 1961), #6.4311.

13. See my *Logical Analysis and Contemporary Theism* (New York: Fordham University Press, 1972) for a defense of theism, consistent with the methodology of conceptual analysis and the tradition of logical empiricism.

14. H. H. Price, *Essays in the Philosophy of Religion* (Oxford: Clarendon, 1972), p. 89.

15. See Richard Rorty, "Mind-Body Identity, Privacy, and Categories," *The Review of Metaphysics*, 19 (1965), 24-54.

16. J. J. C. Smart, "Further Thoughts on the Identity Theory," *The Monist*, 56 (1972), 150.

17. Norman Malcolm, *Problems of Mind: Descartes to Wittgenstein* (New York: Harper & Row, 1971), p. 77.

18. C. J. Ducasse, "The Empirical Case for Personal Survival," *Body, Mind, and Death*, ed. A. Flew (New York: Macmillan, 1964), p. 224.

19. James Cornman, "On the Elimination of 'Sensations' and Sensations," *The Review of Metaphysics*, 22 (1968), 32.

20. Antony Flew, "Can a Man Witness His Own Funeral?" *The Hibbert Journal*, 54 (1956), 242-50.

21. *Ibid.*, p. 246.

22. James Van Evra, "On Death as a Limit," *Analysis*, 31 (1971), 172.

23. Flew, "Can a Man Witness His Own Funeral?" *loc. cit.*, p. 250.

24. See H. H. Price, "Survival and the Idea of 'Another World,'" *Proceedings of the Society for Psychical Research*, 50 (1953), 1-25.

25. Price, *Essays in the Philosophy of Religion*.

26. *Ibid.*, pp. 115-16.

27. See Geach, *God and the Soul*, pp. 17-29.

28. "That the soul remains after the body is due to a defect of the body, namely, death." Thomas Aquinas, *Summa Theologica*, I, q. 90, a. 4, ad 3, *Basic Writings of Saint Thomas Aquinas*, ed. Anton C. Pegis (New York: Random House, 1945), I, 869. "Now nothing unnatural can last for ever: and consequently the soul will not remain for ever without the body. . . . Hence the immortality of the soul would seem to demand the future resurrection of the body." Thomas Aquinas, *The Summa Contra Gentiles* (New York: Benziger, 1929), Book IV, Chap. 79, pp. 270-71.

29. D. Z. Phillips, *Death and Immortality* (London: Macmillan, 1970).

30. *Ibid.*, p. 14.

31. *Ibid.*, p. 44.

32. *Ibid.*, p. 49.

33. I will not deny that ordinary-language idioms lend partial support to Phillips' thesis. For example, we use the locution "he sold his soul to the pleasures of the world," and here we intend primarily to cast aspersion on the moral character of the man, not to describe the bartering activity of some occult ghost in a machine to a metaphorical conglomerate. Furthermore, I do not wish to equate eternal life with endless life, but instead to emphasize the qualitative aspects of such a life. Nonetheless, it makes little sense, if any, to analyse the character of a life *sub specie aeternitatis*, unless death is indeed but an event in such an eternal life, however long one participates in it.

34. *Ibid.*, p. 55.

35. See *ibid.*, p. 58.

36. Augustine, *The City of God*, trans. Marcus Dods (New York: Modern Library, 1950), Book XIX, Chap. 17, p. 697.

Bifurcated Psyche and Social Self: Implications of Freud's Theory of the Unconscious

Leonard C. Feldstein

In this essay, I rethink Freud's theory of the Unconscious. My purpose is not to present a scholarly account followed by an exegesis, but to give an interpretation in the light of my own reflections. When, therefore, I say "Freud says or implies so and so," this is but a shorthand way of saying "the impact of Freud upon me is such and such." Hence, I give an account which, true or false, is, I hope, both plausible and consistent with Freud's thought.[1] Moreover, I indicate, with minimal elaboration, the possibility that this theory allows, in principle, that incorporation of a *social self* in which a deep inner continuity prevails, despite the apparent "solitariness" of the Unconscious, between person and society.

I. introduction

Among the concepts of the psyche developed by philosophers and psychologists, surely the theory of the Unconscious evolved by Freud is the most dramatic and novel. I say this because, contrary to other notions, Freud postulated, and indeed claims to have proved the validity of, the idea of "unconscious" not only as a passive immanent awareness, source of consciousness, matrix of latent mental phenomena, but as, in addition, an *actively* autonomous, systematic, and dynamic organization of non-conscious ideas. Two distinct systems are posed. Though in their interior dynamics these systems are opposed to one another, from the standpoint of the psyche as a whole they are complementary; and by their interplay they are, ultimately in the ideal and rarely achieved instance, unified and transcended. Indeed, only when consciousness and the Unconscious are combined, forming a new product in which each is altered and transformed, is the truth about the *being* of the person revealed. Alone, neither discloses anything but a fragment of that truth. As given, and prior to that interaction which by an inherent *telos*[2] leads, unless hindered by destructive forces, to the sublation of both in a new type of psychic organization, each is in a state of tension with respect to the other; a dynamic equilibrium of tensions ineluctably pervades the psyche. For while each tends to incorporate the other, consuming that other and thereby by a kind of truncation depriving the psyche of its tragic destiny, each at the same time defends itself from the transposition of any of *its* elements into the other. At all costs, the psyche maintains such an economy in this topographic distinction that the integrity of both factors, conscious and unconscious, is perpetuated and resists, save in that rare instance, alteration to the psyche of a Nietzschean *Übermensch.*

Dramatic and novel! For the psyche is construed not as homogeneous and unified but as intrinsically and tragically bifurcated, a tragedy to which the "normal" person is forever doomed. It is the locus wherein unfold two distinct and opposed processes, processes having nonetheless a strange affinity for one another; for each constitutes a symbol[3] whose (latent) meaning is contained within the other. In effect, a double symbology is constructed; for each element completes itself only by combining, and therein finding its meaning, with some element from the opposing system, thereby abolishing the original dissociation. A constellation of symbols of a psyche which in thus duplicating itself thereby dupes itself; and furtively, in its one aspect, conceals what it, in its other aspect, perpetually reveals![4] For it poses itself as *at once* conscious and unconscious, a matrix of meanings both hidden and unmasked. Strange dialectic! A drama enacted by and within the psyche itself! Some of these meanings reside in consciousness; others dwell in the Unconscious. A peculiar symmetry of two contexts of meaning; yet paradoxically an asymmetry in which each (alternately) assumes the guise of "mere" forces while the other the appearance of "true" meanings! Consciousness and the Unconscious are each both *fields of intentions* and *fields of forces*. Freud's theory is, in effect, the theory of this dialectic and the steps by which, through its own dynamism, the confusions it engenders may be clarified.

To proceed: wherever, according to my view of Freud's theory, there is an organism of sufficient complexity to constitute the body of a person, a psyche arises to express the total functioning of that body in its world—a psyche which is, in effect, a reflecting (as sound, sight, smell) of the relationship between its associated body and its world *into* itself. In this self-mirroring or internalizing of that relationship, the organic processes themselves are affected or even redirected. For the human body is an organization of elements so constituted that this organization reflects *into* its own organicity its structure with respect to the structure of the world toward which it comports, incorporating those structures and that relationship as additional organic elements assimilated to previously existing elements. By reflexivity (having its own actions and their consequences for the person turned back upon itself), the body overcomes its status as mere body and becomes, in effect, body spiritualized. For germinating within every *merely* human body is the body of a *person*—an authentically *human* body. More generally, associated with organisms even on the lowest levels of complexity is a self by which that organism leaps beyond itself to possess its own body, to shape in a measure its destiny, and to reconstitute its rhythms.

In the case of a human being, this self is a locus of representations by which the body reconstitutes itself a person and no longer a mere body; for it fashions for itself an image of itself in its relationship to the world. But in every instance this image is a double image. Indeed, every body reflects into itself two images. One expresses that relationship essentially in terms of a body-image, the other in terms of a world-image—though indeed an "imaging" process of one kind presupposes and requires the other kind as condition for its own dynamic unfolding. In particular, in a human body, body ideates doubly; and in this double ideation, it dupes itself as a kind of distorted self-replication. For in its "replica" it conceals from itself how it *really* stands with respect to the world by rendering that "standing" dichotomously. Both members of this dyad must be understood not as merely juxtaposed but as actually synthesized and thus transcended so that the reality of that body in respect to its world is expressed.

In every masking, there is an immanent unconcealing, a disclosure of how an organism stands authentically in its world. Weighed down by a double image and hence with an archaic organicity, each organism tends to overcome its own self-duplicating (i.e., its status as dichotomously conscious and unconscious). This transcendent unity is the synthesizing of body as conscious with body as unconscious. It is body *fully* spiritualized as living its innate and original rhythms as they mesh with the rhythms of the world. In transcendence, body–world resonances are integrated to a cohesive and unified matrix of reverberations. No longer is body the locus of opposing representations. On the contrary, it is a *sublimation*. For mere consciousness—and its correlate self-consciousness—and unconsciousness are sublated in a higher kind of consciousness: one which must, however, be designated by an altogether new term.[5]

I have introduced the notions of autonomy, system, dynamism, complementarity, symmetry, transposition, symbol, duplication, and duping with respect to psychic "ideas" which may be construed as either conscious or unconscious. In the context of my rethinking of Freud's thought, how do I explain these notions? What does it mean to speak of self as locus of a bifurcated psyche? What is this doubly reflexive activity? Wherein consists that unmasking which constitutes authenticity? Further to elaborate this view, and to answer these questions, I treat first the idea of consciousness, then (and in greater detail) that of the Unconscious.

II. CONSCIOUSNESS

What, according to implications of Freud's theory, can *consciousness* mean? Consciousness arises in a context wherein the person orients himself toward an external world which resists his organic activities. This *objecting* to his presence in the world is experienced as an intrusion which must be overcome so that he may organically extend himself into that world. It is as though the organism is wounded by obtrusive stimuli. Its contents pour into the world. Hence, it must defend itself against further threat so that, in its healing, it may continue to function as an integral organism. This healing process is the analogue of consciousness; what protects it (at least initially) "resides" in the analogue to the Unconscious. Hence, a person's activity is so directed that these alien bodies are, for him, negated presences, or are even abolished. By pitting his powers against theirs, he destroys the more *objectionable* objects. Alternatively, depositions (or traces) of their presence may be incorporated or *im*-pressed into his own organic life. In either way, he rejects the world so that it will not reject him. In the latter case, he first *attaches* himself to those objects, even clinging to them by a kind of identification. Then he builds his own identity by detaching himself, gathering into his own organicity their imprints sent forth as radiating stimuli, and internalizing them therein.

Accordingly, the world is *primordially experienced* as, in part, irrational.[6] As such it is a cacophony of stimuli ordered according to no rule inhering within the world itself. On the contrary, it is a chaos of objects which senselessly stand apart from him yet obtrude upon him.[7] What has thereby been received, or "taken back," into his existence (as conscious existence) perishes into that existence.[8] Assimilated, it is thence rationalized. For those "imprints" are synthesized to a self-consistent manifold. Its "center," awareness itself, is focally attended to; and this center fades toward a haunting periphery. A transformation is effected to a context of "images," or a composite of affective, volitional, cognitive, perceptual, and appetitional factors, all unified as a reasonable and harmonious texture. Yet, even as consciousness is constructed by an autonomous dynamism which resides outside of consciousness, it is disrupted by a related but opposing dynamism. The mental factors composing or associated as an *Imago*[9] may actually be dissociated from one another and recombined in such a way as to constitute an altered consciousness.

Once a consciousness germinates "within" the organism, as its mirroring of these external resisting objects to itself within itself, and by their incorporation defending itself against their intrusions, it experiences its own body as analogously constituted by obtrusive factors, particularly when organic pathology transforms them from a well-ordered system to an irrational system, and the person similarly tries to subdue that irrational element by incorporating it, too, as a *body-image*—e.g. kinesthesis. Indeed, this distinction between a well-ordered and a disordered body is similar to an implicit distinction between a well-ordered and a disordered external world. For just as every organism may be attuned to its "healthy" organic rhythms, so it may be in communion with the wholesome rhythms of the external world. By a process only hinted at by Freud, this harmonizing enters consciousness as, on the one hand, a feeling of body vitality and, on the other, an empathy with a world to which one relates rather than which one opposes. For inner and outer worlds, the latter made up of things and persons, are *each* both counterposed to and in affinity with the person. Elements from these worlds are transferred to the body.[10]

An organism of sufficient complexity constitutes itself a person by virtue of its conscious-*ing*. For "consciousness" is, at bottom, an activity and a process. It is the organism as self-directing and self-reforming; the organism projecting itself toward acknowledgment of those "forms" which, in their unity as constituting the unity of consciousness itself, constitute Truth. In every instance, it is associated with a *telos*. Accordingly, the person is one who gathers into systematic unity a schema of the world, inner and outer—in effect, a *cosmology*; and this schema includes interpersonal elements as well as correlative intrapersonal elements. For herein are contained *Imagos* of other persons as not merely organic complexes but as *self*-conscious beings who, reciprocally, incorporate him, in his evolving self-consciousness, into their consciousnesses. By self-consciousness, I mean a person as he consciously searches into his own awareness, discerning hitherto concealed links between its constituent elements. Thereby he incorporates *intra*-personal factors, dynamisms operative "within" his own organicity, which are *un*-conscious. In the cases of both inter- and intra-personal factors, he penetrates the mysteries buried "within" consciousness. He "reads" its imprints as though they were cryptic messages, symbols whose immanent meanings must be drawn forth by consciousness, thereby functioning in a rearranged manifold. Through insight (and inspecting), a consciousness expands until, eventually, it poten-

tiates *itself* to transcend its own condition and to become synthesized with both the Unconscious and the depositions of a
clarified self-consciousness—as Sublimation.

Correlative with its activity of gathering-in *impressions*, consciousness also *ex*-presses those worked-over imprints. It intentionally "stretches" toward the world in gesture, body stance,
vocal inflection. By consciously *re*-attaching himself to external
objects, a person self-consciously reshapes them and thereby becomes artisan, technologist, craftsman, artist, planner, statesman,
scientific experimenter—though the principles or rules governing
these activities are implicit and unconscious. For these now ex-
ternalized objects are *rationalized* as projections of its own content, corporeal symbols of consciousness itself. In its multitude
of movements, body *is* consciousness incarnate. Through dialectical interplay it again internalizes these reconstituted forms.
Consciousness is a continual activity of introjection and projec-
tion. It is also the language through which unconsciousness
speaks; and it, in turn, speaks through the language of body itself. In these ways, the person self-consciously extends himself.
He rearranges his own conscious contents, and thereby alters
both external and internal resistances with respect to which those
contents themselves were formed. Moreover, he transforms his
Unconscious experience, itself constituting a third realm of resistances.

Consciousness is a "mapping" of the world's "surface"; it is
the *creation* of a continuum by way of healing the breach induced by intrusive factors; and it is a *penetrating* of that surface:
to reveal reality concealed within appearance. Through consciousness, the person both masters and communes with the
world. In this complex relationship, by transforming that world
as well as by consuming it, he achieves his authenticity. In addition, consciousness includes *Imago*s as bearing norms and pre-
scriptions. It evaluates these in a quest to reduce inconsistencies
among them, creating a unitary and coherent style of life. Such
directives are initially experienced as counterposed to the person
as resistances. These are absorbed by consciousness in its concept
of the world as a moral order. Unassimilated valuations are con-
signed to the Unconscious wherein they constitute a new psychic resistance. Hence arises the dynamics of the psyche: *Es* (or

indigenous "instincts," an infra-personal world) and *Überich* (a suprapersonal world—the internalized external moral order); against both of these the *Ich* must pit itself by making them reasonable, i.e., by converting them to the rational. For consciousness is the activity of *in*forming the irrational with reason. Thus both *Überich* and *Es* are relegated to the Unconscious, which represents to the self all that cannot be subdued yet must be taken "cognizance of" as alien (even though nonetheless intrapsychic).

Accordingly, consciousness is the *searching I* adjudicating between these interiorized and irrational worlds, themselves in conflict with one another. The world is experienced as perpetually lost to the person, as evanescent; and the terror of this evanescence is relegated to the Unconscious—the scene of a raging battle between its irrational components—while conscious representations enable that abandoning world to be, by implication, mourned by being symbolically won. It is a representing and a refinding of what is absent; what must perish dwells evermore.[11]

The self clings tenaciously to what ineluctably perishes. It seeks to retain it as it was, to arrest it. Yet by binding itself to that world, the self nonetheless transcends it. The integrity of consciousness is preserved. For this integrity is a dialectic between consciousness as integument—a covering sensitive to new stimuli, increasing the intensity of consciousness—and consciousness as integrality, reducing fragmentation to an integer—a whole—and thereby constricting the scope of consciousness. Indeed, consciousness is a precarious balance between these two factors, scope and intensity, expansion and contraction. It is a person as he pulsates in his involvement with the world, resonating to its influences; and as he resonates, he alternates between two poles, just as the Unconscious itself alternates between internalized and indigenous factors; and the self itself exhibits the polarity of consciousness and unconsciousness. Finally consciousness is a truncated "text"[12] which can be completed only by reference to the Unconscious. Delusions must be painfully conquered in order to "transvalue"[13] every given scheme of values. For in its searchings consciousness reveals itself as essentially exegetical; it reads its own cryptic contents by deciphering them in accordance with rules which make themselves apparent only *as* the Unconscious becomes absorbed into an expanding awareness.

III. THE UNCONSCIOUS

On the one hand, Freud *postulates* an unconscious system of "mental ideas" and "affects" as necessary condition for the activity of the self. At the same time, he claims to have *discovered* the Unconscious, both through his examination of his own consciousness—i.e., through a searching into its immanent contents —and by studying the behavior of another and that other's reports about *his* behavior. Hence, Freud proposes two independent ways of ascertaining an actual content for the system whose "existence" as a function of the psyche he initially postulates. For the Unconscious has, he believes, a *mental existence* and is not merely a logical condition for the psychic activities of the person. In the first instance, the criterion is, in effect, the dim apprehension and sudden appearance of mental elements not connected with specific external factors. In the second instance, the criterion is the incongruity of observed behavior with reported behavior. Thus the Unconscious is presumed to be known either by insight or by dissociation—i.e., by naming and feeling what had been unnamed and unfelt; or by experiencing an incongruity, a lack of coherence, a fragmentation. The first is a subjective or phenomenological criterion; the second, an objective or behavioral criterion.

Yet both criteria use a single principle: an irrationality and disconnectedness making itself evident "within" consciousness and "within" behavior. This "making itself evident," or *coming to appearance*,[14] is construed as an activity in accordance with a rule not given in awareness itself, a process whose initial phase is operative unbeknownst to awareness and outside the realm of customary behavior. In one sense, it is close to the *organicity* of the person. Yet it is not intrinsically organic. Rather, it is a matrix of dynamics which intervenes between the organic and consciousness, translating the first into the second. For the Unconscious mediates organic activity. It is the agency for transmitting that activity to awareness and transferring it to overt behavior, thereby reorganizing consciousness and its correlative behavior. In both cases, a "something" is transposed across a barrier. It is a "trans-gression" [15] with respect to that barrier. Moreover, just as consciousness manifests itself in the general contours of organic behavior, and receives its symbolization therein—taking back the "forms" of these symbols into its own contents—so the unconscious symbolizes *it*self in intra-organic behavior. From this point of view, consciousness is a vector which points outward to external behavior; and since that behavior is cohesive with the external world, each interlocking with and configuring the other—where this configuring is a communicating through the sensory apparatus—consciousness indicates the character of external reality. Correspondingly, the Unconscious is a vector which points inward to internal behavior and *its* relationship, via organic boundaries (e.g., osmosis), to the same external world but from within a different perspective. For perspective with respect to a person's relationship to his world is precisely what the bifurcated self conveys, a double perspective where each conceals the other, yet both together constitute the reality of that relationship, i.e., how it stands authentically.

A double vector! And one whose components are themselves vectorially related! For consciousness and the Unconscious are bound inextricably together, cohering in their very opposition, yet drawing apart in their very apposition. In tension, each is locked into the other; and the nature of this "locking in" gives a clue to the character of the Unconscious itself. In this vectorial engaging, each of the other, consciousness mediates, via the Unconscious, the external world to the internal world; and the Unconscious mediates, via consciousness, the internal world to the external world. A double mediation, one which proceeds in reverse directions! For consciousness is a filter through which certain external stimuli pass directly to the Unconscious, as unwholesome for the organism; alternatively, the Unconscious is a filter through which certain internal stimuli pass, and wherein they are contained, "toward" consciousness and hence the external world—containing them, lest both be adversely affected. Accordingly, the Unconscious is the great Container and Protector of stimuli, external and internal. By its activity, a given relationship of the person to the world is, if not authenticated, at least stabilized.

The Unconscious consists of both a content and the dynamisms by which that content is maintained as an integral system. In general, the content consists of two sets of factors: destructive and constructive. Most explicitly delineated by Freud are the former: primary repressions and secondary repressions. But implicit in Freud are the latter: what Jung stresses as archetypal collective "forms," i.e., extra-experiential yet organically rooted ways of organizing experience. The dynamisms include agencies which rationalize consciousness, effect the repressions, transpose elements from the Unconscious to consciousness and, conversely, equilibrate both the Unconscious and consciousness, and redistribute the contents of the Unconscious.

Consider, first, the primary repressions. Freud assumed that stimuli emitted from the body's organs impinge one another, diffusing themselves throughout the organism. Aggregated into patterns, they are brought to focus as a sustained inner activity and organized as *instinct* (viz., *Lusttrieb*—not only sex, narrowly construed, but organ-pleasure or the vitality of the body; *Ichtrieb* —the vitality of the *I* in its self-preserving acts). So powerful are instincts that if unmodified they would disrupt the organism's endeavor to equilibrate itself. Albeit unsuccessfully, it attempts to flee by either mastering or abolishing them. According to Freud, instincts are "mental representatives" [16] of anarchic, intra-organismic fluctuations, exempt from the ravages of time, which would be felt, were they admitted to consciousness, as intolerably painful. Presenting itself to consciousness as a mental idea, the instinct is, however, inhibited from conscious expression, and thus remains unconscious. Though instincts constitute a thrust toward consciousness—their "natural" direction—a counterthrust tends to redirect them toward the organs whence they arose. Yet new organic stimuli counteract the repressed stimuli, keeping instincts in a precarious balance between annihilation and conscious "discharge." Ever falling toward its source, an instinct is depotentiated; its energy-level is de-pressed to a lower level. But repotentiation ceaselessly occurs. Hence, instinct is doubly rejected—by both consciousness and the organ of its origin. This energetic activity causes proliferation of instinctual derivates which, in proliferating, draw into their ever-ramifying network all subsequent repressions; and the web of accretions grows. Protostructural channels (i.e., paths of influence lacking definite morphology) along which new stimuli are led, this weird and complex "fungus" [17] is experienced, protoconsciously, as the haunting, frightening ground of illusion against the resistance of which awareness is endlessly contoured and transfigured. Yet in their loss of energy, in being disallowed re-entry to their organic source, and in proportion to their distortedness and remoteness from the central foci of autonomous, unconscious activity, the furthermost derivates penetrate consciousness as novel forms.

Primary repressions exhibit such properties as specificity, mobility, vacillation, energy exchange, transformation, variability, distortion, redirectedness, circuitousness. A multitude of factors coexists. Ideas and affects detach and reattach themselves in varying arrangements. Depending upon the particular life experiences and organic makeup of an individual, they undergo many vicissitudes. It is not my purpose to trace the details of these processes. But I do stress the potency of such hidden "forces" which, like a magnet, in drawing consciousness into them *deceive consciousness* and trick it into a perverse orientation toward the world. For in varied ways, the Unconscious presses for discharge (i.e., "cathexis") of its energies—originally "mobile" and subsequently, at times, "tonically bound" [18]—by their association with specific objects, external or internal. In part, this displacement is governed by counter-cathexes arising within consciousness and preconsciousness—the region of communication between the Unconscious and consciousness. By such mechanisms as condensation and conversion, the Unconscious is duplicated in consciousness, but in another "state" which, however, represents the same mental content. In effect, a double registration occurs in which the same materials appear (doubly) in two systems, one in the language of the organic (i.e., the instincts, or "frontier" between mental and somatic) and one in the language of consciousness.[19]

Woven into the Unconscious are secondary repressions, depositions of the external world. Filtering through consciousness, though unbeknownst to it, they are excluded from it. For their inclusion would disrupt its rational organization. According to this view, endogenous stimuli are transmitted as a pattern of energy quanta (i.e., organ *Imagos*) toward consciousness. Because of a barrier operative within consciousness itself (a barrier constituted by conscious *forces*), a primary repression occurs whereby the now defective pattern is returned toward its source. But in this process, it is reflected back over the path of its continuing activity. For it encounters anew such patterns of flow. Hence it is again thrust toward consciousness; and, in effect, it

oscillates back and forth, echoing throughout repeatedly coun-
terthrusting stimuli.

This "doubling back" upon itself is a kind of resonance—a
special sort of rhythm akin to but a metamorphosis of the original energy patterns, a rhythm which though a "force" is also
(perhaps latently) "intentional." As other organ stimuli analogously act, these resonances ramify as unconscious experience.
However, "primary process" [20] resonances are not differentiated
in the manner of similar resonances constituting the content of
awareness. On the contrary, they are, *qua* unconscious, a seemingly random chaos of forces. But the designation "experience"
is justified. For in both instances, conscious and unconscious,
resonances are the constitutive element.

Into this maelstrom are woven secondary repressions, i.e., energy patternings of external stimuli. Whereas conscious patterns
are isomorphic with (or duplicate) actual patterns or "forms" of
perceived objects, unconscious patterns are transformations or
distortions to new and grotesque shapes and textures. For herein
is a kaleidoscopic inner world of reconstituted presences, occa-
sionally breaking into awareness as dream, phantasy, overpow-
ering affect. Increasing intensity of such "structured" resonance,
reverberating through continually altered paths of influence, is
associated with a deepening experience. These paths are either
nervous or else those *protomorphic* external channels along which
is conveyed the image of the external world—channels analogous
to internal physiologic ones. Consider the theme of *repetition*.
Habits, familiar ways of approaching the world, are built up,
analogous to impulses traversing nerves as ways of dealing with
the inner world. Indeed, there may be a kind of physiology of
the milieu of the person, less differentiated and, certainly, in
structure incomparably more subtle than the interior channels,
but nonetheless operative. As mobile (interior) energies press for
discharge, resonances crystallize. The system of such loci of in-
terpenetrating resonances corresponds to, indeed is *identical* with,
the sphere of the psyche.

This theory of resonance, implied by Freud, points toward his
endeavor to develop the foundations not only of a physiological
psychology but also of a psychologized physiology of experience. For physiology and psychology imply the same ultimate
concepts—concepts neutral to both disciplines and transcendent

to each. In effect, Freud seeks to create a language into which key terms relevant to both physiology and psychology may be translated. Alternatively expressed: he formulates principles from which physiology and psychology may both be derived. If Freud's own language is physicalistic, and his ideas cast apparently in terms of a Helmholtzian energy model, he is using such language (as when he goes far beyond energistic ideas to such ideas as transference) in a special way; a way which is supraphysiologic and includes the psychologic domain. Accordingly, this is not a theory wherein "experiencing" is reduced to the corporeal, but, rather, a theory where both are jointly reducible to a third realm of being, a realm akin to Spinoza's *substance* as manifesting attributes including mind *and* body.

As a person *relates* to objects in the external world, they in turn relate to him. His very presence before them calls forth, indeed catalyzes, their reciprocal orientation toward him. Not only are they resistances to his expandings into the world and, therefore, the objects of his aggressions, his fruitless demands, so that to be vicariously possessed their *Imagos* are incorporated in his psyche; they also include *persons* with whom he seeks intimacy. Should this quest be frustrated by refusal of either to give himself up to the other in communion, the resultant "distancing" leads to incorporating of traces of these objects as frustrating, negative, hence repellent, stimuli. Drawn by its magnetizing power, they sink into the abyss of the *Unconscious*. Since (and this is a point insufficiently stressed by Freud) the capacity to give is correlative with the need to receive, a system of *internal relationships* develops between hypostatized and introjected "external" (the correlates of the "resonances" previously alluded to) objects. Every new experience yields its quota of such objects which, in effect, inscribe themselves within the already incorporated system, assimilating its features to theirs.

In this process, a potent, self-affirming, and self-integrating *I* becomes fragmented rather than solidified. For it must disperse its energies among the objects of an inner world as well as unifiedly direct them upon objects of the outer world. In its vicarious quest to gratify its need for intimacy, it is, in effect, split into a multitude of *I*'s. Accordingly, a complex, inchoate, uncoordinated, and diffuse *I* oscillates between an interior and an exterior world. So preoccupied is it with the former that to conserve its energies it must use stratagems and deceits to deal with the latter. Yet its inwardly directed activity is, at bottom, unconsummated pseudo-activity. For the inner world is an *Imago* of impotence and rage, i.e., aggression turned inward. It is the locus of *many* centers of partial activity and never a single, unified action. Accordingly, one is free only insofar as (i) the Unconscious (in its negative components) is redintegrated into an expanding awareness, and (ii) the *I* exercises its primordial option of searching into the Unconscious so that its fetters might be removed.

By a play of dynamics so interwoven that each magnetizes the other, this region, too, proliferates and meshes with the realm of the primary repression. Reverberating through the Unconscious is, accordingly, a cacophony of dissociated "voices." The split-up facets of actual objects themselves continue to ramify. For tragically and without end, the *I* seeks among them the *true* objects of its longing. But residing in the exterior world, they have already renounced him or have been renounced by him. Receding from him, they leave in their wake new phantasies. Authentic contact with reality is dulled, impaired, diffused. No longer is reality experienced as fresh and alive, a miracle of powers. No longer does one speak with one's own voice, synchronizing the many voices to a unity. Rather, a distortedly apprehended reality entangles the person in a web of static objects. Either idealized or falsely transmuted to repulsive images, its depositions are seemingly "glued" to his psyche. They refuse to "perish" into an active and continuously regenerated self. As a person flees from one phantasmagoria to another, a psycho-drama of self-deception is continuously enacted. Yet a system of checks and balances maintains these interiorized objects in a specious equilibrium. Inevitably they call forth his futile tactics rather than his direct and efficient action.

Protecting the person from both external and internal dangers, the Unconscious is an evolutionary product of nuclei incorporated as psychic bearers of stimuli, external and internal. Primary and secondary repressions are fused to a dark labyrinth which endlessly generates new and more thoroughly concealed "chambers." By this heightening of tension as the coils of the Unconscious wrap themselves about consciousness, and its several nuclei interact to intensify Unconscious rhythms, unheard organic echoes overwhelm consciousness, or, indeed, break into awareness and conquer it, as in schizophrenia. Yet concealed within these constricting and disintegrating rhythms, when consciousness is sufficiently powerful to counterpose its own rhythms to those of the Unconscious, locking in with them—as when music resonates through one's being and penetrates to its very core—this forbidding womb gives birth to transfigured rhythms, those which are the source and ground of all creative activity. Suffusing consciousness, and thereby transforming it as well as the negative Unconscious, these rhythms enable a new integration to be achieved.

IV. CONCLUSION

In my account, the person has been construed as one who, in self-discovery—as he dwells in a community which, in turn, dwells in him—and with the collaboration of that community, reveals the truth about who he is. Such disclosure occurs through *re-collecting*: a process of gathering into coherence so that he knows he has a history and senses he has a future. In effect, he rebuilds for himself a past, and owns that past. No longer does it haunt him. On the contrary, it reassures him and stimulates his quest for new discovery. The Unconscious is an *in-folding* of imagery deriving from both the external world and his own interiority. Residing within him yet wholly other to him, this Unconscious is a radical negation of all he explicitly is. Yet when deciphered it reveals itself as continuous with his awareness; and by this continuity, each person builds for himself a cosmology of inner and outer worlds as themselves a unity of harmonizing rhythms. By orchestrating the echoes which reverberate throughout the cosmos, he reveals, as an *ontology*, the mystery of his Being in relationship with that of others. Every person is the locus wherein unfolds a multitude of relationships which endlessly spread, interiorly and exteriorly.

The psyche consists of resonances. Its topography is so constituted that it dynamically oscillates between two poles: a small consciousness, a communicating preconscious, a massive Unconscious which coils about consciousness and thereby so intensifies the rhythms of the latter that the psyche must turn toward the other pole; a small Unconscious, a communicating preconscious, a massive consciousness which so coils about the Unconscious that *its* intensified rhythms potentiate a reversal toward the first pole. But should the Unconscious engulf the consciousness, absolute psychopathology (like mob frenzy) prevails. Alternatively, *Unselfconsciousness*—transcendency or authenticity—occurs when consciousness thoroughly absorbs the Unconscious. Yet, in another sense, the Unconscious is a matrix of "archetypal" presences; it is the source not only of distorted presences but of creativity as well—an *endlessly* flowing stream of forces. Moreover, by absorbing the stimuli which *would* break it, the Unconscious protects the finitude, the integrity, of consciousness.

Moreover, each person so affects the other that he incorporates *his* presence which includes unconscious resonances. Through these encounters, by a psychic empathy, the Unconscious of each is itself altered. But the dynamism of this process involves another chapter in the theory of the person: the notions of *transference* and *counter-transference* in the larger context of an ontology of encounter. Fuller account of the Unconscious requires that one take up the problematic of interpersonal relations. Herein it is shown that the distinction between inner and outer collapses. "Nothing is 'without' unless it has passed through and is refracted by the prism of the 'within.' " [21] Yet all that is within is but an echo of that which flows about. The regions of the intrapsychic and the interpersonal are one.[22]

In his speculations, Freud unwittingly and quite unobtrusively shifts from a *narrowly* naturalist concept of the psyche to a personalist and interpersonal orientation. In this shift, the social milieu within which a person dwells becomes not merely relevant but surely constitutive of significant regions of the Unconscious; and this milieu is fused with the elements associated with his instinctual makeup. By so transforming the context of his *stated* theory, the locus of processes wherein the person is deemed *essentially* to be located and from which he accordingly originates, Freud (in the last analysis, for this is the real import of the *Überich*) provides the foundations not only for an "archetypal" (i.e., Jungian) construal of the Unconscious but also for a pervasively social and—I should go so far to say—*transcendentally* naturalistic construal. Beginning with an empirical and a simplistically contrived mechanistic point of view, Freud is led, by the natural movement of his own principles—which would be evident were one fully to make explicit their immanent content—even beyond a naturalism in which its paradoxes and mysteries are acknowledged as *desiderata* for deeper scientific penetration (hence my use of the term "transcendental") toward what is in effect a transcendental *personalism*. But this topic, it must be admitted, Freud does not take up. It remains for those upon whom his theory of the bifurcated psyche has had a profound impact, and who at the same time cannot accept even a humanistic interpretation of Freud's atheism, to assess, develop, and draw forth already latent but quite new meaning.

Freud's discovery of the Unconscious (more accurately, his *re*discovery of what was already perceived by Hegel, and by philosophers long before) has unquestionably led to a revolution, salutary despite its being fraught with certain already prevalent dangers—for what humanist could deny the potential destructiveness of all proposals for human control of human beings, an arrogance so readily overlooked today?—in techniques and approaches to psychotherapy. But a revolution (in a narrow sense) in the art of healing! For, far more significantly, I am convinced, his discovery has immensely enriched a view of the person in which, contrary to many of Freud's own suppositions, *a tenderness of mutual giving*[23] rather than the harsh clashes between and within reciprocally demanding persons will in time assume a central role in any further development of a truly humane idea of an Unconscious—and indeed an idea which is both scientifically valid and philosophically satisfying. I do believe that his theory, true only within far more restricted realms of human conduct than he could have known, entails a notion of sociality which holds that societies of persons dwell within persons, that meaningful interior dialogue is conducted within persons, and that many kinds of social configurations, and an intricate web of relations between their components, are therein internalized.[24] Though not set forth in this essay, my claim is that interpersonal relations reside *within* persons, both a network of deformed fragments of other selves, constituting a strange interior labyrinth, and the imprints of the integrities of other selves.

In conclusion, the concept of "resonances," originally based by Freud upon a neurophysiologic paradigm of psychic activity, entails, I am persuaded, the postulation of a notion of the psyche in which persons, bound to one another by intimacy and empathy, transcending in their communions hitherto unimaginable stretches of space and time, and a notion surely requiring a deep reform of prevailing concepts of matter (a reform which is occurring today in the heart of contemporary physics itself) is thus to be construed: In their sympathetic relatedness, in which each person resonates to rhythms indigenous to the other, while incorporating these rhythms as variations upon those already operative within him, the "center" of each is displaced beyond each, for it lies in the *interstices* of persons, to a transcendent Center, a Center composed of many centers. And *this* Center is that ultimate power of unifying all creatures, both within themselves and between themselves, as the integrity of each and the integrity of all, which alone may be identified (alien as this view is to the view explicitly held by Freud, indeed at the very moment when he strives so vigorously and with the force of his own integrity to annihilate any theistic concept) with the spirit of God.[25] *L'amor che move il sole e l'altre stelle!* [26]

NOTES

1. This article is based on lectures given at Georgetown University in March 1971 and subsequently elaborated on in lectures given at Rutgers University and at the University of Santa Clara in the spring of 1972.

2. My indebtedness to Paul Ricoeur is strong. See his *Freud and Philosophy: An Essay on Interpretation*, trans. Denis Savage (New Haven: Yale University Press, 1970).

3. See note 2.

4. See note 2.

5. See note 2.

6. Freud is never consistent regarding whether this is the way in which the world is, in fact, experienced, or whether, on the contrary, it is thus actually constituted. Roughly, his position would be William Jamesian.

7. See note 6.

8. Whitehead's concept of "perishing" could, I believe, be readily adapted to Freud's theory. See especially Freud's "Mourning and Melancholia," in his *Collected Papers*, trans. Joan Riviere (New York: Basic Books, 1959), IV, 152-70.

9. *Imago* is a term used loosely by Freud, and more by Jung, to designate a composite of perceptual, appetitional, volitional, and cognitive factors which express a particular experience of a particular region of the world, especially of significant other persons.

10. The origin of psychosomatic symptomatology is speculated upon by Freud without being clearly woven into his conceptual framework.

11. See note 8.

12. See note 2.

13. Freud's therapeutic aim—where there is Unconsciousness, so there shall be consciousness—is, I believe, strongly Nietzschean.

14. Heideggerian philosophy, together with Whiteheadian, can, in my judgment, clarify and enrich the general context of ideas within which the Freudian Unconscious can be developed more convincingly.

15. See note 2.

16. Freud's ideas most relevant to this section appear in his "Papers on Metapsychology," *Collected Papers*, IV, 11-170.

17. See note 16.

18. See note 16.

19. See note 2.

20. See note 16.

21. Leonard Feldstein, "Reflections on the Ontology of the Person," *International Philosophical Quarterly*, 9 (1969), 337-38. See also my "Towards a Concept of Integrity," *Annals of Psychotherapy*, 1-2 (1961), 67-87.

22. This is a theme beautifully developed in a manuscript by Dr. Harry Bone which, I hope, will be published posthumously.

23. See the brilliant and little-known work of Ian Suttie, *The Origins of Love and Hate* (New York: Julian Press, 1966).

24. This theme I systematically treat in a book which, I hope, will be forthcoming. See Henry Guntrip, *Schizoid Phenomena, Object-Relations, and the Self* (New York: International Universities Press, 1968); and especially W. R. D. Fairbairn, *An Object-Relational Theory of the Personality* (New York: Basic Books, 1954).

25. For my views on this issue (elsewhere to be presented), my debt of gratitude to my friend Dr. John W. R. Thompson, now deceased, is immeasurable.

26. Dante Alighieri, "Paradiso," *La Commedia Divina*, Canto XXXIII, in *Le Opere di Dante* (Florence: Bemporad, 1921), p. 836.

metaphysics of freedom, time, and history in modern philosophy
was a more genuine expression of Aquinas' vital inspiration than
the Greek objectivism which had been emphasized by classical
Thomistic commentators.

We are hardly surprised, then, that Rahner's philosophical
theology should be marked by its progressive development of
the themes of person and community which characterize modern
German philosophy of the subject. Nor is it any more surprising
that Rahner's development of these themes has been accompanied by the modifications of the more Hellenic elements of his
Thomistic heritage. Rahner's university studies at Freiburg had
given him a keen appreciation of the possibilities which the philosophies of Hegel and Heidegger offered for the development
of Thomism, and, from the beginning of his career, he set out to
exploit them.

Rahner's first philosophical work, *Spirit in the World*, was a
study of Aquinas' metaphysics of knowledge.[2] Although it manifests unmistakably the influence of Maréchal's intellectual dynamism, its starting point is the Heideggerian human subject, the
being-in-the-world who raises the question of Being. This combination of Maréchal and Heidegger was too much for the conservative Thomism of Rahner's mentor at Freiburg, and his
book, which has become a landmark in contemporary Thomism,
was rejected when it was presented as a doctoral dissertation at
the university. The dialogue with contemporary German philosophy became even more evident in Rahner's second book,
Hearers of the Word.[3] Being manifests its luminous self-presence
to the inquiring subject. Yet man, the questioner of being, dis-
covers, through the very dynamism of his question, that he is not
the pure luminous fullness of being. He is a composition of luminous being and the opaque non-being of matter. Still, his un-
quenchable drive to inquire shows that the human spirit is a drive
toward the luminous fullness of Absolute Being.[4] Furthermore,
man could not be the contingent questioner which he is, as being
"thrown into the world," unless he had proceeded from Absolute
Being through the luminously intelligible contingency of an act
of free choice. Man, then, is grounded in the act of love of a
free, personal subject.[5] Consequently, he will understand himself
and his Ground only if he enters into God by responding to Him
through an attitude of free, loving submission.[6] The dynamism

of question thus manifests that being is ultimately both personal and interpersonal.

Rahner not only begins his philosophy by a meditation on the subject; he works out his entire system by using the metaphysics of the person. For him, philosophy, and theology as well, are ultimately anthropologies. Being must be understood as luminous self-presence. The most significant manifestation of being comes through the subject's unobjective grasp of his own spirit and its Absolute Horizon. Being will be truly understood only through a free, loving response, which is, at the same time, the subject's authentic choice of himself.[7] Moreover, the subject is not only free; he is historical and communitarian. The human person is a material knower whose judgments require concepts abstracted from sense knowledge. Although man is a free spirit, open to the Absolute, he is also an incarnate knower, a form received in matter. As such he is a member of a species, who, through his freedom, enters into its communal history.[8]

Rahner's metaphysics therefore is a philosophy of person and community, derived from a dialogue between Scholasticism and German philosophy. Person and community are also the central themes around which he has structured his theological synthesis. By focusing on these themes, and through a brilliant use of the subject's unobjective personal knowledge and the metaphysics of the symbol, both of which are important contributions which his dialogue with Heidegger in *Spirit in the World* made to contemporary Thomism, Rahner has been able to build a powerful theological synthesis around the Holy Mystery.[9] The Holy Mystery becomes the community of the Trinity and, as Rahner's theological anthropology opens out into a Christology, the community of the ontological Trinity is linked to the community of the economical Trinity by his theology of Uncreated Grace.[10] Furthermore, Rahner's philosophy of person and community not only has provided the central structure for his theological synthesis; it has enabled him to make one of his most significant contributions to contemporary theology through his highly illuminating reflections on the free individual in the Church and the modern world.

One need only examine in some detail the use which Rahner has made of his philosophy of person and community to see at once both how important it is in his total synthesis and how indispensable it is to his contributions to ecclesiology, moral theology, and spirituality. The same examination, however, will quickly show a number of difficulties and loose ends which have come to light in the philosophy itself as it has been progressively applied to the increasingly complex problems of contemporary theology.

THE INTELLIGIBLE UNITY OF THE CHRISTIAN MYSTERY

The Christian Mystery, Rahner tells us, does not consist of a collection of truths which our understanding cannot grasp completely in this life, although the understanding will enjoy a penetrating insight into them in the life to come. Such a concept of the Christian Mystery is impossible, for God, the Supreme Existence, can never be grasped through the understanding's objective knowledge. Nevertheless, unobjective awareness of Supreme Existence, the Absolute Horizon of the human mind, is the necessary condition of possibility for all objective knowledge, since Infinite Existence is the goal whose attraction is required to set our human intellect in motion.[11] Moreover, in the historical order, the goal whose attraction stirs the human spirit into movement is not simply God as Infinite Existence. It is the Triune God of grace and glory. Through God's salvific will an offer of Uncreated Grace, the indwelling Trinity, is constantly made to every human soul. Moreover, antecedently to man's acceptance or rejection of justifying grace, Christ's offer of His grace produces an ontological effect in the human soul. This ontological effect is a supernatural existential, through which man's spiritual striving is elevated to the supernatural order. Since his human spirit has been ontologically transformed by the supernatural existential, historical man is now unobjectively aware of the Triune God as the Unlimited Horizon or goal toward which his spiritual dynamism is now directed.[12] Consequently, in the historical order, every human knower can place an act of salvific Christian faith, even though he may remain ignorant of the explicit formulas of Christian revelation. Indeed, historical man cannot fail to do so if, in reverent submission, he implicitly acknowledges the Supreme Mystery, the Horizon of truth and value, in and through his explicit submission to the truth and value of the beings he encounters in the finite world.[13] For, when loving submission to truth and value characterizes man's basic free attitude toward his world and its Horizon, his fundamental intentionality has become a knowing and loving acceptance of the Triune God. When the human person submits his intellect and will, under grace, to the truth and value of the Triune God ontologically present within him, he has implicitly accepted God's personal self-revelation in supernaturally elevated love and knowledge.

Rahner's understanding of mystery liberated him from the "collection of truths" approach to revelation favored by nineteenth-century theologians. In addition, it enabled him to devise a convincing theological explanation of the intrinsic links which bind the individual Christian mysteries together in a coherent, intelligible unity. A more adequate theology of the Hypostatic Union is achieved by bringing to light the intrinsic connection between the Incarnation of the Word and the role of the Word within the Trinity as the expressed Image of the Father.[14] Understanding of this intrinsic connection leads to a clearer appreciation of the connection between God's decrees of creation and redemption. This appreciation in turn gives the theologian a clearer insight into the significance of Christ's salvific will, through which the Word Incarnate offers Uncreated Grace to every man.[15] Uncreated Grace can then become the link which connects our understanding of the ontological Trinity, the inner life of God, with our understanding of the economical Trinity, the Triune God present and acting in the justified soul.[16] Christ through His Incarnation revealed Himself to His community, the Church, to justify the human race by the gift of Uncreated Grace. Thus the mysteries of the Church and the sacraments are intelligibly linked to the mysteries of the ontological and economical Trinity through the saving life and work of Christ.

PERSON AND COMMUNITY IN THE CHRISTIAN MYSTERY

The metaphysics of the person plays an essential role in Rahner's structuring of the data of revelation around what he calls the Holy Mystery. The Holy Mystery cannot be an objective truth. It is the Personal Horizon which, in the historical order, makes possible the spiritual dynamism of every human person. The relations between the Holy Mystery and the human subject are interpersonal. Man's justifying act of faith and love is possible only through an act of loving submission at the deepest level of human freedom. Love, says Rahner, is the light of knowledge. This remains true even when the knower in the Beatific Vision is in immediate proximity to the Holy Mystery.[17] Creation and redemption are understandable only as the result of an act of free love of His creation by the Holy Mystery. Thus the human person himself is essentially a mystery. For man is intelligible only through his drive toward the Infinite Horizon of his love and knowledge. An undeducible free choice of creation and elevation is the ground of man's contingent natural and supernatural being. Incomprehensible value is the eternal lure which forever will attract man's mind and will.

Community is an equally important element in Rahner's structuring of revelation around the Holy Mystery. Rahner's dogmatic synthesis leans heavily on the intrinsic connection which he has established between the ontological Trinity of God's inner life and the indwelling of the economical Trinity in the human soul through Uncreated Grace. In Rahner's opinion—Augustine to the contrary—the ontological status of the Word within the community of the Trinity justifies the older patristic view that the Son alone among the Divine Persons could become man.[18] His theology of Uncreated Grace is intended to provide a more adequate grounding of a presence of God within the soul which is truly communal. Created grace is a work of God *ad extra*. Since works of God *ad extra* proceed from the one divine nature common to all three Persons, created grace cannot provide the ground for a relation of the soul to any of the Divine Persons in His unique hypostatic propriety. Consequently works of God *ad extra* are assigned properly to the divine nature. They are simply attributed by theologians to one or other of the Divine Persons by appropriation. In Uncreated Grace, however, the Persons of the Trinity communicate their proper personal reality to the justified soul. Its ground, therefore, Rahner claims, cannot be an exercise of divine efficient causality, as in the works of God *ad extra*; it must be an exercise of divine quasi-formal causality. Quasi-formal causality alone can be the ontological explanation of the special presence of the Persons of the Trinity in the soul which results in a personal relation of the human spirit to Father, Son, and Holy Spirit in their hypostatic uniqueness.[19] In Rahner's theology of Uncreated Grace, therefore, man becomes a mystery who, in the historical order, can only be understood in terms of his personal relation to the community of the Trinity. The Trinity cannot be a peripheral truth in Christian consciousness. On the contrary, its communal life must be a primordial element in the Christian's understanding of himself and of the world. The community of the economical Trinity is the source of the historical dynamism of the human spirit. Immediate nearness to the community of the ontological Trinity in the Beatific Vision is the goal toward which its historical dynamism tends.

The human community, too, plays an important role in Rahner's structuring of revelation around the Holy Mystery. Man is essentially a mystery because he is a drive toward the Triune God. Yet he is also an incarnate knower, and his movement toward the Trinity must pass through concepts abstracted from sensible reality. A non-intuitive knower, the content of whose concepts must be provided by the senses, cannot be a pure spirit. Man is, therefore, a material and temporal being. As such, he is a member of a species, as is every being whose form is received in matter. As a spatio–temporal subject, man is bound to the history of the world from whose matter his human body has evolved. As an historical subject, man cannot express even his most intimate thoughts without using the language of his community. And so he can achieve his personal fulfillment only through interaction with the fellow-members of his culturally determined society. Objective knowledge is possible only through concepts, and conceptual knowledge of the world is not simply the product of direct abstraction. It is also, as we are increasingly aware, the product of the cultural development of the historical linguistic communities in which concepts are formed and used. Therefore, the development of man's personal relationship to the Trinity in knowledge and love requires the mediation of his historical community.

Man's membership in an historical community is also the reason why historical revelation is possible. God can speak a word of revelation to man because God is the Holy Mystery who, if He chooses, can freely manifest His inner life to man. Man is capable of hearing God's revealing word because he is a dynamic knower who can thematize his knowledge of the Absolute Horizon of his spirit, albeit in an inadequate and analogous manner, through the concepts which he abstracts from sense experience.[20]

Since man is an historical being and a member of a species, he should not be surprised if a word of revelation should be expressed through human concepts at a definite time and place in the history of his race, and that it should reach individual men through the mediation of the human community.[21] Should such an encounter with historical revelation occur, the unthematic knowledge, which the justified soul possesses of the Absolute Horizon of its world through its loving response to finite values, could be clarified by the explicit objective knowledge of this historical revelation. Implicit faith could then be transformed into explicit faith, and, to use the words of J. B. Metz, transcendental revelation could be clarified and supplemented, though not eliminated, by categorical revelation.[22]

REVELATION AND THE CHURCH: THE DIALECTIC OF PERSON AND COMMUNITY

The dialectic of transcendental and categorical revelation carries over into the dialectic of the individual and the Church. The objective word of historical revelation is a manifestation, through the limping, analogous knowledge mediated by concepts, of God's hidden personal depths. Historical revelation thematizes and clarifies the unobjective knowledge which the human knower possesses of the Trinity through his loving submission to the values of the world and its Absolute Horizon. Yet objective revelation in its turn can be accepted only through loving faith. The historical word of revelation demands for its salvific reception a human soul in whom the Triune Mystery dwells through Uncreated Grace.[23] Loving submission to the Triune Holy Mystery through the conversion of faith and charity is required of the Christian knower who desires to penetrate the true essence of the objective revelation mediated through Scripture and Tradition. Listening to the word of God involves a dialectical interaction of transcendental and categorical revelation.

Rahner's dialectic between transcendental and categorical revelation in the converted Christian is an expression in contemporary terms of the traditional dialectic between knowledge of God by connaturality and knowledge of God through the objective word of Scripture and Tradition. This is, of course, a dialectic which goes back to patristic times. It is implied in the whole "ascent to wisdom" tradition associated with the patristic and medieval theology of the image of God in man. Bonaventure, who shares Rahner's conviction that the Trinity is the key to a true interpretation of reality, relies on it to structure the stages of the soul's ascent to the Supreme Truth and Good in his *Itinerarium mentis in Deum*. Bernard Lonergan employs it to justify the central position which he assigns to conversion in *Method in Theology*. Without personal knowledge of the personal God, illuminated by the light of love, there may be an exercise in the history of ideas, but there can be no theology. Objective knowledge, however scientific, must always be nourished by the interpersonal encounter of the individual Christian person and the Holy Mystery. Without the unobjective experience of this personal encounter, objective knowledge of God by the very nature of the case must be deficient as knowledge.

Nevertheless, the objective word of revelation has a normative character which may not be disregarded. Uncreated Grace, the ground of transcendental revelation, is intrinsically connected with Christ's salvific will. Christ's salvific will in its turn is intrinsically linked to the Incarnation. By His Incarnation, the expressed Image of the Father, who alone among the Persons of the Trinity could do so, "became other" when He expressed Himself corporeally through the human body which He united to His person. Christ, as man, is at the same time the ontological manifestation of the Godhead and a member of the human race. As such, He belongs both to the divine and to the human communities. Uniting Himself to human history as the definitive ontological manifestation of the divine community, Christ is a communal word spoken to the whole human race. Therefore both His word and His grace require a definitive and indefectible historical community, which will abide as the visible sign and locus of His active presence and remain the custodian of His objective word of revelation.[24]

Consequently, Rahner sees the saving event of revelation as intrinsically connected with the formation of the Christian community. Revelation closes with the death of the last apostle because that event marks the definitive formation of Christ's Church.[25] Transcendental revelation comes to all men, and we find more or less adequate objectivizations of it in all the higher religions.[26] Nevertheless, as we have seen, a definitive, identifiable community must always remain in existence as the custodian of Christ's historical word of revelation. However small and scattered that Church may be, it will always have the task of presenting the explicit word of revelation to each generation. The Church must live and act as the community of Christ's visible presence within the larger community of anonymous Christians in whom Christ lives through Uncreated Grace. She will always be the sign raised among the nations. Her explicit word will always be needed to thematize and clarify man's unobjective knowledge of the Trinity within him.

As a member of the human race, every man must accept the restrictions imposed on his individual freedom by his dependence on the human community to which he belongs.[27] He cannot express his implicit knowledge of God without thematizing it in some way through objective words and culturally conditioned gestures. Neither can he express his implicit love of God without mediating it through his love and reverence for his fellow-men and their personal and communal values. Similarly, the converted Christian cannot express his knowledge and love of the Triune Mystery without using the words, symbols, and gestures of the community of Christ's visible and tangible presence and activity. Nor can he neglect the legitimate demands which the Church imposes on him in virtue of his membership. The Christian's relation to God cannot be authentically personal without also being communitarian. The Christian, in whom the community of the Trinity dwells by Uncreated Grace, will reach immediate nearness to the community of the ontological Trinity in the Beatific Vision by recognizing the values and accepting the legitimate demands of the worldly and ecclesial communities. For such is the law of the human and divine communities.

COMMUNITY AND THE METAPHYSICS OF THE SYMBOL

Person and community are thus the structural elements through which the central elements of Rahner's theology are linked together. As we have already seen, Rahner has used the distinction between the knower's conceptual knowledge and his unobjective awareness of its Absolute Horizon with great fruitfulness. This distinction, as we have also seen, underlies Rahner's new concept of the Christian Mystery. Again, by exploiting the spirit's awareness of its Horizon, Rahner has been able to unite his theology of the supernatural existential and of Uncreated Grace to his theology of transcendental revelation. Through his use of conceptual knowledge, on the other hand, Rahner has linked his theology of historical revelation to his theology of the individual member's relation to temporal society and the Church. Both forms of knowledge have been employed with great effect in Rahner's theology of the development of doctrine, in his epistemology of moral and spiritual discernment, and in his critique of contemporary ideologies. The dialectic between unobjective and objective knowledge and the interplay between individual commitment and communal responsibility run through Rahner's handling of all these themes.

Now that we have seen how essential Rahner's philosophy of the person is to his whole synthesis, we can understand more readily why he insists that theology is an anthropology. Not only does Rahner's theology begin with a reflection on the fundamental intentionality of the human spirit; it develops its major themes by using a metaphysics based on an analysis of human knowledge and love. Indeed, Rahner's further claim that theology is an anthropology which opens out into a Christology could hardly be made unless his theology was structured by a metaphysics based on the metaphysics of the human person.

The role assigned to Christ in Rahner's theological synthesis rests on the validity of his claim that the Word is the real symbol of the Father. A real symbol, in Rahner's understanding of the term, is a reality which proceeds from its ontological source in such a way that, although it is really distinct from it, it remains united to its source in the unity of a single ontological reality. Thus, for example, the intellect and will are real symbols of the human soul. As proper accidents, they are really "other" than the soul, the source from which they emanate. Yet they remain united to the soul in the unity of a single subsistent being. Therefore the soul can "express itself" through its existence and operation in its faculties of intellect and will. Maintaining its own essential unity, it reaches the fullness of its being through its existence in these "others," its proper accidents.[28] In an analogous way within the Trinity, Rahner claims, the Son, as Word, is the real symbol of the Father. Although He retains His primordial unity as Source, the Father "expresses Himself" in His Image, the Son. Through His relation of intellectual generation to the Son, the Father becomes aware of His own personal identity as Father. Then, knowing each other, Father and Son are joined in the loving unity of the Godhead by the Spirit.[29]

The Son is thus the supreme theophany, the Personal Revelation of the Father. Consequently, He alone of the Persons of the Trinity can become a Personal Revelation of the Father through a Hypostatic Union. Furthermore, a Hypostatic Union is possible only with a human nature. God can use many creatures as the instruments of His transient activity. But only man can be the real symbol in whom the Son can *personally exist* as in His other.[30] For man alone, among earthly realities, is the contingent mystery whose spiritual dynamism is a drive toward union in knowledge and love with the Absolute Mystery. Therefore the more man gives himself to God, the more he realizes the possibilities of his own human nature. Consequently, man will realize himself most fully when he gives himself completely to God through personal identity. Theological anthropology opens out into Christology when we realize that the ultimate possibility of human fulfillment is that man can become the real symbol in whom the Son exists through the Hypostatic Union.

Human nature, as the real symbol of the Son, as we have already seen, links the Word Incarnate to the history of the human race and of the Church. The metaphysics of the symbol, moreover, makes it possible for Rahner to explain more fully the relations between these two societies.[31] When a real symbol proceeds from its ontological principle, it retains its own identity, even though it is ontologically united to its source. The body, as the real symbol of the soul, retains its ontological identity, even though the soul comes to perfection by existing in it as its form. Likewise, the natural order of creation, which proceeds from redeemed and elevated human nature as the latter's real symbol, retains its independence and autonomy, although it remains united to the order of grace to form one order of redemption. Thus Christ, the Redeemer, through His gift of Uncreated Grace, exists in the sacramental order of His Church through her preached words, rites, and sacramental symbols. But He also penetrates the natural order of creation as the Absolute Future, the goal toward which the evolution of its history is directed.

Church and world, therefore, are related, though autonomous, realities. For her thematization of the word of revelation, the Church is dependent on the historical development of human concepts in the context of human culture and society. Human society in turn is protected by the teaching of the Church from the ideologies which, during the present century, have confused the finite realities of race or state with the Absolute Future, who alone is the ultimate object of human hope and human striving.[32]

The metaphysics of the symbol can also clarify the relation of the free individual to each of these societies. Rahner's metaphysics of the person has revealed that there is no such thing as a purely individual reality. Every being comes to perfection by expressing itself in its "other." This is true through the whole range of being from the lowliest material particle to the Supreme Community of the Trinity. Inanimate bodies express themselves, through their transient activity, in other material beings. Man expresses himself by going out to the material world in sensation and by responding to his world and its Horizon in knowledge and love. The Persons of the Trinity express themselves through their personal relation to each other. Thus the metaphysics of the symbol makes it evident that individual and community are correlative terms. They are also analogous terms, since the relation between individual and community varies on the different levels of being. Forget their correlative character, and you fall into the error of individualism. Forget their analogous nature, and you fall into the error of collectivism, which uses the model of the biological organism to define the relation of every individual to his community.[33]

Since the human person must express himself on many diverse levels in his interaction with his world, he finds that he is a member of many communities—the biological, the economic, the cultural, the social, the religious. As a human person, the individual expresses himself through his free response to the hierarchy of values. In doing so, he defines himself in his relation to the hierarchy of communities in which these values are incarnated.[34]

PERSON AND COMMUNITY: RESPONSIBLE DISCERNMENT

The human person, therefore, must reach his perfection by responding to the hierarchy of communal values. Human freedom is not an arbitrary, individual power. Rahner is clear in his assertion that both civil society and the Church have genuine authority. His ontological grounding of the status of community validates the right of the state and the Church to require obedience to their legitimate legislation. Both may, and indeed must, impose legitimate restrictions on the freedom of their individual members. Situation ethics has no appeal for him.[35] His belief in the validity of conceptual knowledge has convinced him that there are universal principles which can serve as valid objective norms for moral action. Nevertheless, the relation of the free individual to the Absolute Horizon of his world brings him into personal confrontation with the Triune God. Loving surrender to God does not always consist in the exact fulfillment of universal obligations. God can make demands of the individual which, although purely personal and directed to the individual alone, still constitute true obligations.[36]

Furthermore, since personal surrender in love to God is the supreme fulfillment of the human person, this interior personal surrender, rather than exact exterior observance of communal regulations, should be the aim of moral and religious direction.[37] Those who possess authority, especially in the Church, should always be mindful of this important fact. They must school themselves to respect the initiative of free individuals who on their part are obliged to follow the personal commands which they receive from God. The community of the Church must assist its individual members to discern God's personal inspirations correctly and to follow them freely. Furthermore, the Church's rulers must never forget that the individual Christian is a member of a hierarchy of communities. Prelates must not try to arrogate to their remote, central bureaucracies the pastoral decisions which should be made by the diverse sub-communities which have a legitimate existence within the larger community of the Church.[38]

Rahner's reputation in the early days of *aggiornamento* was due in large degree to his brilliant use of the interplay of unobjective and objective knowledge in his theology of the free individual in the Church. His essays on situation ethics, the charismatic and hierarchical element in the Church, free speech and public opinion in the Church, religious obedience and the discernment of spirits, received wide and favorable attention. Although they are still extremely influential and deservedly so, these essays by no means exhaust Rahner's theology of moral and religious discernment.

Membership in the visible Church is important in Rahner's eyes for moral and spiritual discernment. The Church is the visible, tangible sign of Christ's presence. She is, in a special way, the locus of Uncreated Grace. In the Church there exists what Rahner calls the *a priori* of Tradition, the Church's indefectible loving surrender to the Triune Mystery.[39] In the Church the word of revelation is unfailingly heard by a faith illuminated by love. Thus the Church possesses a personal knowledge of God which surrounds her objective thematizations of revelation as an unobjective "fringe." The Church's objective thematization of revelation develops as concepts and their contexts change through cultural evolution. Nevertheless, the Church's indefectible personal knowledge of the Triune Mystery, through the *a priori* of Tradition, is her guarantee that, despite logical discontinuities, her doctrinal formulations are always expressions of the same Mystery.[40] Furthermore, although concepts and their contexts change, we are not in a situation of complete conceptual relativity. A number of our basic concepts are thematizations of the perduring fundamental structure of the human person. Principles expressed in these concepts are not subject to the flux of history. It is possible, therefore, for the Church's magisterium to use such changeless concepts in her infallible thematization of the Christian Mystery. Thus the individual Christian is aided in his moral and religious discernment both by his participation in the loving submission of his community to the Triune Mystery and by the infallible directives of her magisterium.

The Christian must be more modest in his expectations today, however, than he was in the past. The number of changeless concepts is more limited than we used to think, and, as a result, the number of changeless infallible pronouncements must be correspondingly limited. Likewise, the power of the Church to guide man's temporal activity has been radically restricted by our growing appreciation of the complexity of nature and the culturally determined character of temporal realities. In the past, the Church confronted the world of nature. The cycles of the seasons and the structure of society were fixed realities which seemed "always to have been there" and to have "come from the hand of God." Man's place in the world of nature and society was stable and well-defined. It was easy to find the will of God in conformity with social and familial obligations which were generally recognized. Furthermore, the range of human knowledge was limited. Even in the eighteenth century, one man could master the body of literary and scientific information which constituted society's knowledge of "God and His world." Church and state knew where they were, and it was relatively easy for king, prelate, and individual to define their relations to one another.[41]

Today, however, that relatively simple and stable condition no longer exists. The growth in man's technical ability has now brought the world of nature under his control. Nature, even human nature, is no longer to be simply accepted "as it comes from the hand of God." It has become the ambiguous subject of human manipulation and human choice, with all the possibilities for evil and error which lie in human action. Society and culture are no longer simply "natural." They, too, are recognized products of human manipulation. Furthermore, the range of human science has become so great today that a single individual can no longer master it. No man today possesses adequate knowledge of the world which man has produced or of the society in which man lives. Due to the vastness and complexity of human knowledge, the diverse intellectual and technical communities which constitute the modern world can no longer communicate with one another.[42]

Thus the individual Christian, who is a member of many communities, is now in a difficult position. He lives in an age of philosophical pluralism in which no sage can adequately unify our knowledge of temporal realities. He must make moral decisions in a world which the vastness and complexity of human technique have made ambiguous.[43] His Church can give him no firm and detailed guidance about social and scientific processes which she herself does not understand. Yet there are important services which she can render him. Through her commitment to the Absolute Mystery, the Church preserves him from the ideologies of the age.[44] The Church's "faith instinct," her ability to discern values which she possesses in virtue of her loving submission to the Horizon of all values, still enables her to give illuminating

pastoral directions in the grave situations in which the fundamental values of the individual and society are threatened.[45]

Nevertheless, the individual Christian is thrown more on his
own resources than he has ever been in the past. Although he
has been taught by philosophy and by revelation that he is communitarian by nature, his relation to the diverse communities of
which he is a member has become ambiguous. If no man today
can understand the totality of these communities, no man can
master the relationships among them. And, in a world in which
even human nature seems subject to technical manipulation, the
metaphysical grounding of the hierarchy of the various communities is called into question. Even within the Church, fruitful
intercommunication between the various sub-communities and
the whole community of the Church seems to be impossible. The
expansion of human knowledge has led to philosophical pluralism and to the autonomy of the natural and human sciences.
Philosophers can no longer communicate with one another; and
scientists cannot communicate with philosophers. Given the existence of this situation, it is no longer possible for the magisterium to teach and guide the Church, as it did in the past,
through its use of one basic, universally accepted system of philosophy. Rulers and members of the Church must reconcile
themselves to the fact that, in large areas of their existence, often
those which concern them most vitally, the members of her diverse cultural, intellectual, and technical sub-societies are no
longer able to communicate with one another.[46]

This is a rather ironical conclusion for Rahner to have reached
in his later writings. It is rather depressing that a theologian,
whose whole synthesis has been built upon community, must
now admit that man's ability to lead a communitarian life has
become so limited. Rahner himself, however, professes no dis-
couragement at this discovery. Man's communitarian life, he
thinks, can make up in its increased intensity for its diminished
scope. The human person is defined through his drive in knowledge and love to the Absolute Mystery. That dynamism both
defines his dignity as a free individual and presents him with the
challenge to achieve personal fulfillment through his submission
to the realm of value. Men must concentrate their attention today
on those basic elements of personal existence which bind them

all together as men. Reverence for the vast areas of other men's experience, into which they cannot hope to enter, can be a form of communication. Silence, after all, is a form of speech. Return to the Mystery, the Absolute Horizon of all forms of objective knowledge, must be the path to communication between men when the unbridgeable diversity of their scientific and philosophical conceptual systems have divided them. And in this return to the Mystery, Christians, moved by the economical Trinity within them, the community of Uncreated Grace, should lead the way. Rahner sees in this return to the Mystery the road to the creation of a united Christian community, whose fundamental faith could be thematized in a very limited number of formulated teachings, and in which great cultural and theological diversity would be permitted.[47] He has not, however, spelled out in any detail how this new unity and diversity would enable individual Christians to define their position in the Church and in the world.

RAHNER'S PHILOSOPHY OF PERSON AND COMMUNITY

Rahner's remarkably unified synthesis and his wide-ranging and illuminating reflections on the relationship of the individual Christian to the Church and to the modern world have grown out of his philosophy of the person. His frequently quoted dictum that theology is an anthropology is a very accurate description of his own theological writings. They are, in fact, a brilliant expansion and application of the metaphysics of man which Rahner worked out in his early philosophical studies, *Spirit in the World* and *Hearers of the Word*. Rahner's philosophy is fundamentally a metaphysical anthropology grounded by a transcendental reflection on the conditions of possibility for human knowledge. In his understanding and use of the transcendental method, Rahner is a consistent Transcendental Thomist. His theory of knowledge and his epistemology of the concept and judgment are unmistakably Thomistic. So is the metaphysics of matter and form, essence and existence, which emerges from his epistemological reflection on human knowledge. Rahner is following the lead of Maréchal when he accounts for both the abstraction of the concept and the assent of the judgment through the intellect's natural drive toward Infinite Being. He is continuing the Maréchalian tradition when he proposes the metaphysical composition of act and potency in the finite being as the fundamental condition of possibility for human knowledge.

Nevertheless, as we saw at the beginning of this essay, Rahner has also been influenced by contemporary German philosophy. Whereas Maréchal confined his dialogue with German philosophy to a confrontation with Kant and the great post-Kantian Idealists (whom Rahner by no means neglects), Rahner's philosophy shows the effects of his own dialogue with the early Heidegger. The influence of Heidegger can be seen in Rahner's stress on Infinite Being as the conscious, though unobjectively grasped, Horizon of the knower's world. It also appears in the weight which Rahner places on freedom and history in his philosophy of the human person, and in his stress on the Holy Mystery as the necessary condition for all objective knowledge.

No one can deny the immense service that Rahner's metaphysics of the subject, which emerged from his effort to absorb the early Heidegger into his own Thomistic system, has rendered to theology. Without it his restructuring of theology around the ontological Trinity and the economic Trinity would have been impossible. It is essential to his concept of theology as an anthropology which opens out into a Christology. It is also indispensable for his brilliant theology of the individual and the community. The question remains, however: is it adequate to the task which Rahner has assigned to it?

PROBLEMS WITH RAHNER'S PHILOSOPHY
OF PERSON AND COMMUNITY

The crucial questions connected with Rahner's philosophy of person and community concern his transcendental anthropology. Does his transcendental method establish a sufficient number of abiding truths to serve the function which it must serve in Rahner's philosophy of person and community? Indeed, does it establish the very fundamental truths without which Rahner's essential understanding of man and society cannot be validated?

From the early days of his theological activity, Rahner has admitted that his transcendental method cannot ground by itself a sufficiently wide range of general principles to support his natural-law ethics of the individual and society. It must be supplemented by other principles derived from an empirical study of man in his contingent historical development. Rahner has never departed from this early position. Yet his growing emphasis on the complexity of modern technology and on the historical element in human knowledge and human nature gives his readers an uneasy feeling that the task of combining *a priori* principles grounded by transcendental anthropology with empirical principles derived from an empirical study of man may be becoming difficult to the point of practical impossibility. Indeed, Rahner's more recent writings on philosophical pluralism and on the autonomy of the natural and social sciences do not make encouraging reading for the social ethician. Social philosophy, it seems, if it wishes to retain its universal character, must confine itself to a severely limited number of directives. Might it not turn out, after all, that the limited practical return from Rahner's philosophy of society hardly justifies the rigorous reflective efforts which his anthropology demands?

Furthermore, even though Transcendental Thomists may be willing to agree with Rahner that the Horizon of the human spirit is Infinite Being, Heidegger is by no means willing to agree with him. Heidegger says emphatically that, for him, Being, *Sein*, is not the Infinite God; and Heidegger's understanding of the historicity of man and his world is more radical than Rahner's Thomistic adaptation of it. In Heidegger's phenomenological ontology, man is not ordered to the Infinite Pure Act of Existence, much less to the community of the Trinity. There is need for a much more detailed and protracted dialogue between Heidegger and Rahner in order to ground clearly and securely the understanding of the Horizon of the question of being on which Rahner's theological anthropology is built.

Even if Rahner can establish his fundamental metaphysical point that the human mind is a drive to Infinite Being, his account of conceptualization can still cause difficulty for a number of his readers. Rahner insists stoutly that his philosophical anthropology has shown that there are abiding concepts whose content is not subject to the flux of history. On the basis of the existence of such concepts, he justifies his theological position that the Church can make a limited number of irreformable infallible pronouncements. However, other theologians have sharply challenged this assertion.[48] Consequently, Rahner's teaching on the

origin and nature of the concept, which is essential to his ecclesiology and his moral theology, requires more careful grounding.
Rahner's early treatment of conceptualization went little beyond
a Maréchalian account of the abstraction of an intelligible form
from matter on the basis of the dynamism of the mind. In his
later writings, he has shown a growing awareness of the culturally conditioned origin of human concepts and of the historical character of their content. Unlike Bernard Lonergan, however, he has done little to unite these two aspects of his writing
on conceptualization in a single coherent position.

Again, Rahner has moved very rapidly at times when he rec-
onciles elements taken from other philosophies with his own essentially Scholastic metaphysics. His "supernatural existential,"
on which his theology of implicit faith and the anonymous Christian has been constructed, has evidently been inspired by the
existentialia, or dynamic universal structures, of Heidegger's
Dasein. Yet the exact role played by this "Heideggerian existential" in Rahner's Scholastic metaphysics of grace and the supernatural has puzzled a number of his commentators.[49] Other commentators are not sure that Rahner is being metaphysically coherent when he attempts to absorb a Hegelian insight into his
Scholasticism through his metaphysics of the symbol. Can Rahner really say, on the one hand, that God is the Thomistic Pure
Act of Being, and still claim, on the other hand, that God follows the Hegelian dialectic and truly "becomes other" in the real
symbol of Christ's human body?[50] Yet, if Rahner cannot make
this claim, a great deal of his most influential and inspiring writing about God's real involvement in the history of the human
community is deprived of its metaphysical basis.

Rahner's prolific and brilliant work in expanding and applying
his philosophy of person and community has prevented him from
returning to his earlier work on its epistemological and metaphysical foundations. We cannot expect a great theologian to do
everything. Rahner has constructed one of the richest and most
highly unified theological syntheses of this century. He has focused theology and spirituality on the Trinity and the Incarnate
Word more sharply than it has been focused since the time of
Bonaventure. He has made an immense contribution to moral
theology, ecclesiology, and the theology of temporal realities.
His disciples have continued the application of his philosophical

anthropology to the diverse areas of Catholic theology. Let us hope that other disciples will direct their attention to the loose ends and difficulties which weaken Rahner's epistemology and metaphysics in their present state. The legitimate questions which these difficulties have provoked from other theologians must be answered if Rahner's theology is to continue its fruitful contribution to the Christian community. In this work of philosophical reflection, Rahner's disciples should be aided by the reflections on the foundations of theology recently published by his fellow-Thomist Bernard Lonergan.

NOTES

1. Johannes Baptist Metz, *Christliche Anthropozentrik* (Munich: Kösel, 1962).

2. Karl Rahner, s.J., *Spirit in the World*, trans. W. Dych, s.J. (New York: Herder & Herder, 1968).

3. Karl Rahner, s.J., *Hearers of the Word*, trans. Michael Richards (New York: Herder & Herder, 1969).

4. *Ibid.*, pp. 53-68.

5. *Ibid.*, pp. 83-91.

6. *Ibid.*, pp. 96-102.

7. *Ibid.*, pp. 101-105.

8. *Ibid.*, pp. 129-30.

9. "The Concept of Mystery in Catholic Theology," *Theological Investigations* IV (Baltimore: Helicon, 1966) pp. 36-73, esp. pp. 63-73.

10. *Nature and Grace* (New York: Sheed & Ward, 1964), pp. 125-41.

11. "The Concept of Mystery in Catholic Theology," pp. 37-44.

12. "Concerning the Relationship Between Nature and Grace," *Theological Investigations* I (Baltimore: Helicon, 1965), pp. 297-317, esp. pp. 308-14. For an excellent discussion of the supernatural existential, see Kenneth D. Eberhard, "Karl Rahner and the Supernatural Existential," *Thought*, 46 (1971), 537-61.

13. "Anonymous Christians," *Theological Investigations* VI (Baltimore: Helicon, 1969), pp. 390-98. For a good discussion of Rahner's theology of the anonymous Christian, see Anita Röper, *The Anonymous Christian* (New York: Sheed & Ward, 1966). See also "Reflections on the Unity of the Love of Neighbor and the Love of God," *Theological Investigations* VI, pp. 231-49.

14. "Current Questions in Christology," *Theological Investigations* I, pp. 149-200.

15. "On the Theology of the Incarnation," *Theological Investigations*

IV, pp. 105-20, and "History of the World and Salvation History," *Theological Investigations* v (Baltimore: Helicon, 1966), pp. 97-114.

16. "Some Implications of the Scholastic Concept of Uncreated Grace," *Theological Investigations* I, pp. 319-46.

17. "The Concept of Mystery in Catholic Theology," p. 41.

18. "The Theology of the Symbol," *Theological Investigations* IV, pp. 221-52, esp. pp. 235-37.

19. "Some Implications of the Scholastic Concept of Uncreated Grace," pp. 329-33.

20. *Hearers of the Word*, pp. 140-49.

21. *Ibid.*, pp. 150-63.

22. *Ibid.*, p. 67n10.

23. "Considerations on the Development of Dogma," *Theological Investigations* IV, pp. 3-35, esp. pp. 11-15 and 30-31.

24. "Freedom in the Church," *Theological Investigations* II, pp. 89-107, esp. p. 96.

25. "Considerations on the Development of Dogma," pp. 9-10.

26. "Christianity and the Non-Christian Religions," *Theological Investigations* v, pp. 115-34.

27. "The Dignity and Freedom of Man," *Theological Investigations* II, pp. 235-63.

28. "The Theology of the Symbol," pp. 222-35. See also *Spirit in the World*, pp. 253-60, and *The Christian Commitment* (New York: Sheed & Ward, 1963), pp. 44-46.

29. "The Theology of the Symbol," p. 236.

30. *Ibid.*, pp. 239-40, and "On the Theology of the Incarnation."

31. *The Christian Commitment*, pp. 38-74.

32. "Ideology and Christianity," *Theological Investigations* vi, pp. 43-58.

33. *The Christian Commitment*, pp. 75-82.

34. "The Dignity and Freedom of Man," pp. 238-41.

35. *Nature and Grace*, pp. 49-59, and "On the Question of a Formal Existential Ethics," *Theological Investigations* II, pp. 217-34, esp. pp. 217-20.

36. "On the Question of a Formal Existential Ethics," esp. pp. 226-29. See also *The Dynamic Element in the Church* (New York: Herder & Herder, 1964), pp. 13-41.

37. *The Christian Commitment*, pp. 108-11.

38. "Peaceful Reflections on the Parochial Principle," *Theological Investigations* II, pp. 283-318.

39. "Considerations on the Development of Dogma," pp. 24-27.

40. "The Development of Dogma," *Theological Investigations* I, pp. 39-77, esp. pp. 63-74.

41. *The Christian of the Future* (New York: Herder & Herder, 1967), pp. 39-76.

42. "A Small Question Regarding the Contemporary Pluralism in the Intellectual Situation of Catholics and the Church," *Theological Investigations* vi, pp. 21-30.

43. "Philosophy and Philosophizing in Theology," *Theological Investigations* IX (New York: Herder & Herder, 1972), pp. 46-63. See also "The Experiment with Man," *ibid.*, pp. 205-24.

44. "Ideology and Christianity," *Theological Investigations* VI, pp. 43-58. See also "Marxist Utopia and the Christian Future of Man," *ibid.*, pp. 59-68.

45. See note 41. See also "The Problem of Genetic Manipulation," *Theological Investigations* IX, pp. 225-52, esp. pp. 236-43.

46. See notes 42 and 43.

47. See note 43.

48. The existence of changeless concepts was one of the elements of Rahner's celebrated debate with Hans Küng on infallibility. For a good account of this debate, see John Jay Hughes, "Infallible? An Inquiry Considered," *Theological Studies*, 32 (1971), 183-207, and Georges Dejaifve, s.j., "Un débat sur l'infallibilité. La discussion entre K. Rahner et H. Küng," *Nouvelle Revue Théologique*, 103 (1971), 583-601.

49. See William C. Shepherd, *Man's Condition* (New York: Herder & Herder, 1969), pp. 85-93. See also note 12.

50. See Joseph Donceel, s.j., "Second Thoughts on the Nature of God," *Thought*, 46 (1971), 346-70, esp. pp. 351-52 and 364-65.

5

Person and Technology:
A Deweyan Perspective

ROBERT J. ROTH, S.J.

TECHNOLOGY HAS FALLEN UPON HARD TIMES in recent years. It has been indicted in whole or in part for the slum conditions of our cities, for the pollution of our natural resources, and for our military involvement in foreign countries. As a consequence, many Americans have serious reservations about the role of technology as it affects civilization and culture, and one hears more and more frequently the charge that technology is bringing about the death of the human person.

Hard questions are being raised on a broader scale as well. What does America stand for? What are the ideals, aims, and purposes which are to give meaning to our very existence and which should enable us to grow according to the inherent dignity of the human person? What is it in our past tradition that we judge worthy to be fostered and developed today, and what is it that we would hope to pass on to future generations? Have we clearly formulated in our own minds the contribution which America can make to the growth of human beings here and in other parts of the world? In the past, we have tried to do this by slogans, like Manifest Destiny and New Freedom, the New Deal and the Fair Deal, the New Frontier and the Great Society. But these today seem all so pretentious, so quaint, so antique, even though some of them are hardly a decade or two old. It should be a warning to us that yesterday's slogans can become today's shibboleths, that the catch-words which inspire us today may be the object of derision tomorrow, and that today's prophet may be tomorrow's fool.

And yet, we cannot do without prophets who will authentically interpret the present and give guidance for the future. Perhaps we need slogans, too, for man is a maker of symbols. But the real question is: Who is the genuine prophet, and what are the symbols which have enduring value? Not everyone who stands up and says "I am alienated" becomes by that act a prophet, though a sense of alienation may well provide the background for prophecy. But the question remains: "Who is the real prophet?" This is an agonizing question, and my reason for raising it is not to deride prophecy or symbol, but to underscore the difficulty of discerning which are the valid ones.

It is debatable whether John Dewey is the prophet the present generation needs. What cannot be denied, however, is that two decades after his death he is still America's best-known philosopher and educator. Moreover, during a teaching career of more than fifty years he was no ivory-tower intellectual. He believed that the philosopher should be engaged in the human clash of social purposes and aspirations. Problems of poverty and disease, social justice and the underprivileged, the dignity of the human person and the possibilities for the development of human potentialities—all these were important to him. Consequently, he was anxious to assist in the improvement of the institutions which concerned themselves with these issues.

It should not be surprising, then, that Dewey gave serious thought to the problems of science and technology. Hence, in view of the powerful influence which his ideas exerted on so many aspects of American life, it would be well to review what this philosopher had to say about the possibility of the growth of the human person in an age of technology. What we can expect from philosophical reflection are not detailed solutions to the many problems which face modern technology but general principles which in whole or in part can give guidance in the formulations of these solutions.

THE GROWTH OF TECHNOLOGY

When John Dewey began his teaching career in 1883, technology was still struggling for recognition and acceptance in America. We are told that the word "technology" was coined in 1829 by a Harvard professor named Jacob Bigelow.[1] But long before that, England had supplied the model for technology, as meaning the application of the physical sciences to industry. Prior to the American Revolution, the colonies had had little opportunity to develop industry. In fact, they were discouraged from doing so by the British Parliament, which wanted to preserve the character of the colonies as a rich source of raw materials for its own industry and to maintain the dependence of the colonies on the mother country. It should be pointed out, however, that in their reaction to the Sugar and Stamp Acts of the 1760s the colonists gave early evidence of their potential for developing industry by boycotting colonial imports of British manufactures and succeeding, on a small scale at least, in producing manufactures of their own.

After the Revolutionary War, the new republic was faced with the explicit question whether or not it should maintain the rural, agrarian character of the country and depend on imports from England, or develop industry after the British model. One of the most vigorous defenders of the agrarian ideal was Thomas Jefferson. In his *Notes on the State of Virginia*, first published in 1785, he argued from moral grounds. In praise of the agrarian life, he wrote:

> Those who labour in the earth are the chosen people of God, if ever he had chosen people, whose breasts he has made his peculiar deposit for substantial and genuine virtue. It is the focus in which he keeps alive that sacred fire, which otherwise might escape from the face of the earth. Corruption of morals in the mass of cultivators is a phaenomenon of which no age nor nation has furnished an example.[2]

On the other hand, Jefferson saw in an industrial economy the seeds of corruption. He stated:

> The mobs of great cities add just so much to the support of pure government, as sores do to the strength of the human body. It is the manners and spirit of a people which preserve a republic in vigour. A degeneracy in these is a canker which soon eats to the heart of its laws and constitution.[3]

For these reasons, Jefferson advocated that America send its raw materials to Europe rather than bring back corrupt manners and principles. He was aware that such a procedure would seriously limit the economy of the new republic, but he judged this sacrifice worthwhile in the light of the political, moral, and religious values which would be preserved.

Although Jefferson to the end of his life maintained this position as an ideal, he soon came to realize that in practice it could not be achieved. For one thing, it would make America too dependent on England. For another, he admitted in a letter that his fellow-countrymen had "a decided taste for navigation and commerce. They take this from their mother country." [4] Moreover, realistically he had to take into account the natural ambition of men to get ahead and to improve their economic condition. In view of all this, he acknowledged that America would some time engage in full-scale commerce and industry, though he believed that that day would be distant. This was an opinion shared by not a few statesmen of the day, and John Adams could write to Benjamin Franklin in 1780 "that America will not make manufactures enough for her own consumption these thousand years." [5]

But a thousand years were quick in coming. In fact, it took scarcely half a century. According to Leo Marx, the situation in 1829 was as follows:

> A profitable factory system was firmly established in New England; new roads and canals and cities were transforming the landscape; on rivers and in ocean harbors the steamboat was proving the superiority of mechanized transport, and outside Baltimore *the* revolutionary machine of the age was being made ready for use: thirteen miles of the first important American railroad, the Baltimore and Ohio, were under construction. . . . Between 1830 and 1860 the nation was to put down more than 30,000 miles of railroad track, pivot of the transportation revolution which in turn quickened industrialization, . . . the economy was expanding at a remarkable rate, the new technology was proving itself indispensable, and the nation was on the verge of the "take-off" into the era of rapid industrialization. [6]

By the first half of the nineteenth century, then, America was well on the way toward the development of a technology in advance of any other country in the world. It was like the uncoiling of a giant spring, though the analogy may tend to exaggerate somewhat the gradual rate of development in its earlier stages. Nonetheless, it was as though all America was poised for some such moment. For there were seemingly limitless supplies of raw materials. There was also an abundance of human energy and ingenuity which, in a remarkable way, had been characteristic of the colonies from the very beginning. These were mobilized under the added impulse to prove what could be accomplished now that Americans had gained their independence. From one perspective, it would seem that the drive toward industrial development had gained the day and that the Jeffersonian ideal had been washed away before the swelling torrent of enthusiasm.

But this, too, would be an exaggeration. It would be to forget, for example, the New England transcendental movement prior to the Civil War. This was a very complex movement, and George Whicher oversimplified it when he called it a "revolt against materialism." [7] It was much more than that, for it was a very crucial step in the breakdown of Calvinistic Puritanism in America. But Whicher is correct when he writes:

> The transcendentalists were deeply concerned about the quality of life in America. A great tide of material prosperity . . . had overtaken the country. Everything was expanding by leaps and bounds. Virgin territories were being opened to settlement from Illinois to Oregon. Turnpikes, canals, steamboats, railroads were rushed into being. . . . It was an era of good feeling, a time when the common man seemed to be getting his share of creature comforts. Yet sensitive observers feared that all was not well. It appeared not unlikely that care for man's intellectual and spiritual nature might be submerged in the rush for easy riches. What would be the profit in all this material advance if it were not matched by an equal progress in humanity? So the transcendentalists pondered.[8]

If one remembers nothing else from reading Henry David Thoreau's *Walden*, surely he will recall Thoreau's annoyance when, while sitting along the peaceful shores of Walden Pond, he heard the shrill cry of the nearby railroad train:

That devilish Iron Horse, whose ear-rending neigh is heard throughout the town, has muddied the Boiling Spring with his foot, and he it is that has browsed off all the woods on Walden shore, that Trojan horse, with a thousand men in his belly, introduced by mercenary Greeks! Where is the country's champion, the Moore of Moore Hall, to meet him at the Deep Cut and thrust an avenging lance between the ribs of the bloated pest?[9]

It would be a mistake to see in these remarks merely the petulant impatience of a man whose idyllic peace and quiet had been disturbed. In prophetic manner, Thoreau sees in the railroad a symbol of the machine which threatens to control the destinies of men. For he says:

We do not ride on the railroad; it rides upon us. Did you ever think what those sleepers are that underlie the railroad? Each one is a man, an Irishman, or a Yankee man. The rails are laid on them, and they are covered with sand, and the cars run smoothly over them. They are sound sleepers, I assure you. And every few years a new lot is laid down and run over; so that, if some have the pleasure of riding on a rail, others have the misfortune to be ridden upon.[10]

PERSON IN COMMUNITY

It would be relatively easy for us to go through the literary and religious writings of the nineteenth century and to draw from them similar warnings against the growing industrial development of the age. It is sufficient for us at present to recognize that it was in the midst of this attitude that John Dewey began his academic career. From the very beginning he tried to assess the role of technological and industrial development. What role should technology play? Is it favorable to the growth of the person, is it hostile, or is it merely neutral? Dewey knew the stock objections which were being raised against technology, so it was not a problem he could ignore. But he adopted a position which was not to change throughout his long life; it was a position favorable to technology.

Before we attempt to describe Dewey's attitude toward technology, however, it is necessary first to explore a bit his understanding of person in relation to community. This would require a long discussion in itself, but it is possible, I think, to isolate elements which Dewey would consider essential to the question. His dominant preoccupation, and indeed the dominant motivation behind his entire philosophical enterprise, was to determine the conditions according to which the individual might reach his highest fulfillment as a human person.[11] No matter how detailed or technical his discussions could become—whether they dealt with education, technology, psychology, political theory, or whatever—the central issue was the attempt to answer the basic question: In what does man's highest fulfillment consist, and what are the conditions according to which this ideal may be achieved? His answer was that the peak of human fulfillment consists in the total dedication of the individual to the betterment of his fellow-man and in the direction of all his energies to the enrichment of the lives of others. This ideal entails self-sacrificing effort for all men, those who are living in the present and those who will come after us. In the awareness of solidarity with all mankind, and in the exertion of effort in its behalf, man reaches his highest fulfillment.

This ideal implies that members of the community share common goals and purposes. All of them appreciate the value of human fulfillment and dedicate themselves to its achievement. Without this, "any so-called social group, class, people, nation, tends to fall apart into molecules having but mechanically enforced connections with one another."[12] Moreover, the members cooperate in using those means which are best calculated to achieve the goal in view. United in aim, they are also united in effort, and they experience the solidarity of pooling their resources and efforts in striving for a goal they hold in common. The result is a true community, which is found "wherever there is conjoint activity whose consequences are appreciated as good by all singular persons who take part in it, and where the realization of the good is such as to effect an energetic desire and effort to sustain it in being just because it is a good shared by all."[13]

But there is something more to community living than a community of goals and activities. A group of people may agree regarding the goals they should be seeking. But they might strenuously object if they were denied the opportunity to exercise their freedom, responsibility, imagination, and emotions in selecting those activities which best lead to the attainment of the goals which have been chosen. Without this opportunity, Dewey maintains, "minds are warped, frustrated, unnourished by their activities"; there is a "complete separation of mind and body . . . and the result is a depressed body and an empty and distorted mind." [14]

With Dewey's notion of community as a background, we are better able to appreciate his favorable attitude toward technology. It goes far beyond seeing in technology a means of affording man the possibility of improving his physical condition. Certainly Dewey is not closed to this. It is an exciting prospect to think that man's ability to control material resources could be the means of removing poverty and disease and of assuring for all a measure of material comfort. These are not inconsiderable advantages.

Beyond this, however, is the opportunity which technology affords of uniting mankind into a true community. Industry by its very nature leads to corporate, and one should even say cooperative, action on a wide scale, for it brings together a large number of individuals, working on a common enterprise, sharing and communicating methods and techniques, and using common instruments of work. In this respect, one might say that our technological age is unique in history for it goes beyond any other age in providing the opportunity for people of all walks of life to dedicate their intellectual and physical energies to the common enterprise of improving the lot of mankind.

Other considerations may be added here. For example, modern travel and communication have caused the world to shrink in time and space so that almost in an instant we can be present in body and spirit in almost any part of the world and share in the experiences of peoples of other nations and traditions. Their concerns become ours, and we learn very quickly that, in spite of the many characteristics which differentiate people, we are remarkably alike in our hopes and aspirations. It is a commonplace to say that modern methods of communication have literally broken down the walls between countries and nations. Even those who live in physical isolation become aware of the larger community which transcends distance.

One could idealize at this point, but the endeavor to land men on the moon is a classic example of the union of aims, interests, and efforts, not only of the vast number of people actively engaged in the enterprise, but, literally, of the people of a whole nation and of large parts of the world who can watch its progress with more than a passing sense of involvement and commitment. Here we see taking place what happens in the relatively narrow range of the scientific community where many inquirers are working on common problems, participating in joint operations as a team, and sharing their solutions with others for the continued progress of science. American philosophers who share in Dewey's ideal of reaching human satisfaction through community action have been impressed by such considerations as these, and they have concluded that the pursuit of scientific knowledge provides a paradigm case of community endeavor in contemporary life.

DISADVANTAGES OF TECHNOLOGY

So much for the advantages Dewey sees in technology. Actually a defender of our technological society would not be hard-put to draw up a litany of praise in its behalf. We have at hand countless objects which are the result of technology and which serve our needs. But what about its disadvantages? These too are many. And so, like Satan who can quote Scripture on both sides of any question, we too could cite both the advantages and the disadvantages of technology. We all know that technology is a mixed blessing, but the difficulty is to decide whether or not the mixture destroys the blessing.

Lewis Mumford has long been a critic of American culture. In 1926 he endeavored to underscore America's preoccupation with commercial power and economic gain after the Civil War. He wrote:

. . . industrialism had entered overnight, had transformed the practices of agriculture, had encouraged a mad exploitation of mineral oil, natural gas, and coal, and had made the unscrupulous master of finance, fat with war-profits, the central figure of the situation. All the crude practices of British paleotechnic industry appeared on the scene without relief or mitigation.[15]

Mumford repeats this theme in a more recent book in which he predicts that in the future age of "megatechnics," "man will become a passive, purposeless, machine-conditioned animal." [16]

Herbert Marcuse, too, from a Marxist position, has criticized modern technology.[17] In his view, American culture and her political and economic system have been so dominated by the machine that Americans have become incapable of criticizing present ideals and purposes or of projecting new ones for the future. Without realizing it, our citizens gradually lose their freedom to choose other alternatives, and those who strive to do so are considered to be dangerous or at best useless. If we grant the accuracy of Mumford's and Marcuse's analyses of the contemporary scene, they would serve to provide literal verification of the evils which Thomas Jefferson foresaw, even if somewhat dimly, at the end of the eighteenth century.

Now, as a matter of fact, Dewey was familiar with the main criticisms of technology, for they had appeared in one form or another many times and with increasing acrimony since the days of Jefferson. Moreover, his long life spanned the period of America's more significant and rapid advances in technology. During that time, he had witnessed the burgeoning of city life with all its ills. He had direct contact with settlement houses which dealt with the problems of the poor and underprivileged. He lived for extended periods in large cities, and he knew well the problems of poverty, disease, social injustice, and racial prejudice. He lived through two World Wars and the atom bomb. In short, he had seen Thoreau's Iron Horse grow into a Frankenstein's monster. In his less optimistic moments, he even conceded that Jefferson's fears had been more than justified.[18]

Many times, then, Dewey put before himself the question "as to whether the material and mechanistic forces of the machine age are to crush the higher life," or again, "can a material, industrial civilization be converted into a distinctive agency for liberating the minds and refining the emotions of all who take part in it?" [19] As we have seen, his answer to both these questions was one favorable to an industrial civilization. But this answer must be understood only in terms of his theory of community. In assessing what was wrong with industrial society, he maintained that at the root of its ills was the dominant concern of the modern American for his own private financial interest, with the consequent loss of social awareness or concern for all men based on a profound respect for the human person. As a result, our industrial society, instead of providing the conditions for the expression of common goals and interests, the exercise of shared activities, and the expansion of human ingenuity and imagination, had become the arena for the drive to private wealth and power, for the repression of human freedom and responsibility, and for the exploitation of the masses leading to the material aggrandizement of the few. In Dewey's view, then, it is not the machine which is at fault but the man who uses the machine; it is not the industrial society as such which is to blame but the community of men who have allowed selfish aims to dominate their lives. But Dewey felt that if human relationships were motivated instead by a sense of social awareness, then modern technology would indeed be "a distinctive agency for liberating the minds and refining the emotions of all who take part in it."

Dewey believed also that we are born without an appreciation for the value of social awareness. Hence the child as early as possible should experience for himself the value of social living. That is why the lived experience of cooperative activity formed such an essential and indeed exciting part of his educational theory and practice.[20] For Dewey, education must fulfill the vital role of giving the young the experience of living in community. But he criticized American education for fostering intellectual immaturity regarding social problems—in a passage found, not in a work on education, but in a book on political and social theory.

This immaturity is mainly due to their enforced mental seclusion; there is, in their schooling, little free and disinterested concern with the underlying social problems of our civilization. Other typical evidence is found in the training of engineers. Thorstein Veblen—and many others have since repeated his idea—pointed out the strategic position occupied by the engineer in our industrial and technological activity. Engineering schools give excellent technical training. Where is the school that pays systematic attention to the potential social function of the engineering profession?

I refer to the schools in connection with this problem of American culture because they are the formal agencies for producing those mental attitudes, those modes of feeling and thinking, which are the essence of a distinctive culture. But they are not the ultimate force. Social institutions, the trend of occupations, the pattern of social arrangements, are the finally controlling influences in shaping minds. The immaturity nurtured in schools is carried over into life. If we Americans manifest, as compared with those of other countries who have had the benefits of higher schooling, a kind of infantilism, it is because our own schooling so largely evades serious consideration of the deeper issues of social life; for it is only through induction into realities that the mind can be matured.[21]

If as much attention were given to passages such as these from Dewey's works as is given to what he says about sandboxes and field trips, we might have a more balanced and authentic picture of his educational theory.

THE FUTURE OF TECHNOLOGY

There is one more pressing question which must be faced when one considers technology. It is this: is the advance of technology inevitable? In other words, no matter how much we may theorize about its advantages and disadvantages, is it true that technology will continue to advance? I am not aware that Dewey himself ever explicitly faced that question. Hence in answering it, I shall be giving what I *think* Dewey's response would be, though in all honesty I will have to take full responsibility for any criticism which may be leveled against that answer.

I would have to argue that the advance of technology *is* inevitable, that America and the world will become *more* technological and not less so. I would base that judgment on several considerations. First of all, there seems to be at the root of the American temperament, explain it how you will, the irrepressible urge to find better, easier, and quicker ways to get things done. It was Thomas Edison, I believe, who is supposed to have said: "There's a better way of doing it; go and find it." From one point of view, the history of American technology could be written as an expression of that statement. I am not sure that this urge is limited to Americans, but I certainly feel that it is characteristic of their whole approach to life. No doubt this tendency is often exploited for financial reasons. But the main point is still valid. Why settle for less—whether it involves moving across the ground, over a river, or through the air; whether it means making a pair of shoes, a container, or a truck? "There's a better way of doing it; go and find it." To me, it is inconceivable that the day will ever come when Americans will rest content to take things as they are as long as there are better ways of doing things.

But I believe there is something deeper at work here. Any philosophy student is familiar with Aristotle's dictum: "All men by nature desire to know." This profound statement has become a cliché through repetition, but it is important that we do not obscure the basic insight. Many factors go into the explanation of man's development throughout his long history. Some of these factors are intimately bound up with the need for bare survival. But we do not go very far in our explanation unless we take into consideration man's desire to uncover the secrets of nature. Without this urge, we would have had no civilization, no culture, and indeed no science. The mysteries of nature have provided the challenge to man's mind, and it is due to the ceaseless urge to know that he has advanced in his knowledge and control of nature.

Not long ago people used to say: "Some day man *will* reach the moon." That man *did* reach the moon is hardly an argument for prophetic or psychic powers on the part of those who made such a statement. It is a simple inference from what we know about man's past: not only about his great facility in manipulating instruments and machines, but more importantly about his desire to know, to find out, to force nature to yield its secrets. Of course, one may argue that the main motivation behind the moon landings was the desire to maintain American supremacy over Soviet Russia in the race for space, or that the vast sums of money expended could have been better used for improved housing and health services at home. I would not care to dispute the first objection when it is applied to those who shape governmental and military policies. And there is good reason to argue that the amount of money spent on moon landings was not justified in terms of more pressing problems. Yet that man should have gone to the moon at all is largely due to the teams of scientists and technologists who are interested in the pursuit of knowledge and who need only the financial resources necessary for such a pursuit.

We have said, then, that the drive toward the development of technology is one manifestation of the drive of the human mind to know. Might we not push the matter one step farther? Might we not even look upon this drive to know, and this drive to develop technology, as a manifestation on the human psychic level of the basic thrust of evolution? As a process, evolution forged ahead through advances and regressions until it reached the state of man. Might we not see technology as a step in that development, an age which has never been seen before, but which has been prepared by slow and steady growth and which bears the seeds of new meaning for the future? New evolutionary forms never emerge full-blown and perfect on the first try; they come forth hesitantly, ill-shapen, poorly developed, with many blemishes. It is only through struggle, pain, and even loss that they mature to the full potential which is in them.

Can we realistically say, then, that technology can be halted, or severely limited? I think not. For I cannot imagine how it would be accomplished. It would mean the forceful suppression of activities which have endured for a good many years, in a good many areas of the world, by a good many people. The prospects of this suppression are not a little frightening, for it would take a more powerful force than Thoreau's hoped-for gladiator to "thrust an avenging lance between the ribs of the bloated pest." It would require gigantic social upheavals. And after powerful forces have been unleashed, I fear that the end result would resemble the attempt to put out a raging forest-fire with a lawn sprinkler.

But then, suppose that technology really turns out to be a Frankenstein's monster; suppose that man has lost control and that, like a wild machine, technology is on the rampage, threatening to destroy us all. That, too, is a frightening prospect. Some do not at all hesitate to say that this is a literal description of the stage which modern civilization is fast approaching.

Frankly, I find it difficult to share this pessimism. I still believe that there are resources within the human person which will enable mankind to move beyond the ill-formed state of evolution which it has now achieved. But this will not happen automatically. And that is why I am also convinced that, whatever further dimensions may be needed in his position, Dewey was on the right track. The main lines of that position have been indicated in this paper. In many respects, the theme will perhaps sound all too familiar, for it is one which is being developed currently in other philosophical movements, as well as in psychology, sociology, political theory, and even in religious and liturgical sources. Hence Dewey has no monopoly on these ideas.

It is to Dewey's credit, however, that, long before others were aware of the problem, he developed a full-blown social and political theory applicable to many aspects of modern life, including technology. The theoretical models which he confronted were those of Rousseau and eighteenth-century libertarianism, as well as *laissez faire* social and economic theory bolstered by the deterministic Darwinism of Herbert Spencer. One would have to explore these dimensions of Dewey's thought to appreciate his position fully.[22]

But central to it all was the fact that he placed the hope of the future upon the commitment of all men to their mutual development as human persons within a community. On the positive side, contemporary criticism of technology can be looked upon as a step on the part of American society toward that commitment. In Dewey's terms, it remains to make that commitment more explicit.[23]

NOTES

1. Leo Marx, *The Machine in the Garden: Technology and the Pastoral Ideal in America* (New York: Oxford University Press, 1967), p. 149. I have drawn heavily upon this excellent book for my treatment of Thomas Jefferson.

2. *Ibid.*, pp. 124-25. See also Thomas Jefferson, *Notes on the State of Virginia*, ed. William Peden (Chapel Hill: University of North Carolina Press, 1955), pp. 164-65.

3. Marx, *Machine in the Garden*, p. 125.

4. *Ibid.*, p. 134.

5. *Ibid.*, p. 148.

6. *Ibid.*, p. 180.

7. *The Transcendentalist Revolt Against Materialism* ed. George F. Whicher (Boston: Heath, 1949).

8. *Ibid.*, pp. v-vi.

9. Henry David Thoreau, *Walden and Other Writings of Henry David Thoreau* ed. Brooks Atkinson (New York: Modern Library, 1959), p. 174.

10. *Ibid.*, p. 83.

11. I have developed this aspect of Dewey's thought in my *John Dewey and Self-Realization* (Englewood Cliffs: Prentice-Hall, 1962).

12. John Dewey, *Freedom and Culture* (New York: Putnam, 1939), p. 12.

13. John Dewey, *The Public and its Problems* (New York: Holt, 1927), p. 149.

14. John Dewey, *Individualism Old and New* (New York: Putnam, 1930), p. 132. From the previous discussion, it should be evident that for Dewey culture includes all those aspects of contemporary life which contribute to the highest fulfillment of the human person. His fullest treatment of the relation of technology to culture is given in his works on social and political theory cited earlier; namely, *The Public and its Problems, Individualism Old and New,* and *Freedom and Culture.* Another important book which should be included is *Liberalism and Social Action* (New York: Putnam, 1935).

15. Lewis Mumford, *The Golden Day: A Study in American Experience and Culture* (New York: Boni & Liveright, 1926), p. 159.

16. Lewis Mumford, *The Myth of the Machine: Technics and Human Development* (New York: Harcourt, 1966), p. 3.

17. Herbert Marcuse, *One-Dimensional Man: Studies in the Ideology of Advanced Industrial Society* (Boston: Beacon, 1966).

18. John Dewey, *Freedom and Culture,* p. 8.

19. John Dewey, *Individualism Old and New,* pp. 123-24.

20. John Dewey, *Democracy and Education* (New York: Macmillan, 1916), p. 3; *The Public and its Problems,* p. 154.

21. John Dewey, *Individualism Old and New,* pp. 127-28.

22. See the works of Dewey cited in note 14. For my own interpretation of Dewey's social and political theory as related to technology, see my *John Dewey and Self-Realization,* pp. 50-62. For a good discussion of how Dewey applied his own theory to an active engagement in politics, see the unpublished doctoral dissertation of Edward J. Bordeau, "The Practical Idealism of John Dewey's Political Philosophy" (Fordham University, 1969), and Bordeau's "John Dewey's Ideas about the Great Depression," *Journal of the History of Ideas,* 32 (1971), 67-84.

23. John Dewey, *A Common Faith* (New Haven: Yale University Press, 1934), p. 87.

6

Individual and Society:
A Whiteheadian Critique
of B. F. Skinner

Elizabeth M. Kraus

INTRODUCTION

"SOCIETY" FOR ALFRED NORTH WHITEHEAD is a metaphysical term referring to a special mode of togetherness exemplified in a group of individual entities[1] which are mutually implicated in each other.[2] As a metaphysical term, it is not directly descriptive of the complex of relationships called "society" in ordinary language. It is far too general a category to be used for purely descriptive purposes. However, given the applicability demanded by the first of the pragmatic criteria for a speculative scheme,[3] and given Whitehead's insistence that "everything of which we are conscious, as enjoyed, perceived, willed, or thought, shall have the character of a particular instance of the general scheme," [4] human social relationships and human society as such ought to be interpretable as special cases of the metaphysical category. They are particularizations of the general, embodying it in much the same way as a biological species embodies the general characteristics of the genus to which it belongs: not in a univocal manner, but in a way in which the general acquires depth, richness of content, and full determinateness through its instantiations. This is to say, in another language, that a universal can become particular through its incarnation in concrete, existential circumstances without at the same time losing its metaphysical generality.

To take Whitehead's speculative sociology as an interpretative framework within which to examine human society is, in his own image, to land the airplane after its flight into the stratosphere of metaphysical generalization.[5] In the landing, the metaphysics is verified (or falsified), having been "confronted with the circumstances to which it should apply," [6] and the experience itself becomes more lucid, having acquired "an enhanced penetration by reason of the expectation evoked by the conclusion of the argument." [7] "The facts are known with more adequacy and the applicability of the system to the world has been elucidated." [8]

This essay will attempt such a landing with respect to "society," taking as its restricted area the relation between individual and society, and as its limiting problem the apparent conflict between personal autonomy and social control which has led B. F. Skinner to maintain through the mouth of *Walden II*'s Frazier:

> . . . in the long run man is *determined by the state*. A *laissez-faire* philosophy which trusts to the inherent goodness and wisdom of the common man is incompatible with the observed fact that men are made good or bad and wise or foolish by the environment in which they grow.[9]

I. METAPHYSICAL SOCIOLOGY

The notion of society in Whiteheadian metaphysics is not an incoherent addition to the theory of actual occasions; rather it arises from that theory as a natural consequence. Each actual occasion represents for Whitehead the growing together or "concrescence" of all reality (past or possible, fact or form) to produce the drop of experience, the quantum of space–time which constitutes the emergent occasion as a novel perspective on the universe. Historical fact and atemporal form are welded together to yield a moment of private enjoyment. The interfusion resulting in that private unity is not to be viewed as a merely additive process which would render the unity of an occasion comparable to that of a sum. Each element in the data out of which the occasion arises is grasped [10] in a feeling[11] qualified by a subjective form[12] which makes the prehension integrable with the manifold of other prehensions involved in the concrescence,[13] the subjective form being determined by the subjective aim[14] of the concrescent subject. What results, therefore, is a unification of the multiplicity of public facts in the emerging occasion, a unification which is both organic and private. The completed or "satisfied" subject has assumed a perfectly definite relation toward every element in the universe and has realized a unique, unrepeatable, and "personal" perspective, which then, under various aspects of its determinateness,[15] becomes part of the public data for future concrescences.

What is being maintained in the theory regarding the self-realization of an occasion is a theory of internal relations, in which each element of the universe is viewed as inextricably bound up with every other element. It is not the case for Whitehead that an entity is some determinate thing-in-itself or already constituted substance which relates itself *per accidens* to the rest of the universe. On the contrary, what an entity is in itself is precisely the synthesis of the activities whereby it organizes the many into a private perspective.

> . . . the word "subject" means the entity constituted by the process of feeling, and including this process. The feeler is the unity emergent from its own feelings; and feelings are the details of the process intermediary between this unity and its many data.[16]

The feeler does not antedate its feelings; neither does it endure in its subjective immediacy when the process of feeling is complete. Subjectivity perishes into objectivity; the subject is superjected, thrown forward, as an objective datum for future feelings, demanding future syntheses.[17]

> The world expands through recurrent unifications of itself, each, by the addition of itself, automatically recreating the multiplicity anew.[18]

Therefore, any object felt by a concrescent subject is not a bare "it" waiting to be related to other bare "its"; it is already a superjected unification of the facts in its past, which themselves were syntheses of their past. It is this vision of "nature *in solido*" which dominates and names the philosophy of organism. Each entity is what the others make it to be; each entity reflects the entire universe, is the macrocosm in microcosmic perspective. This togetherness of mutually implicated occasions forms the groundwork for Whitehead's metaphysical sociology, for society is merely a special case of the primordial interfusion of reality.

A nexus of occasions is termed social when, in addition to the mutual immanence of its members, each embodies a common form or "defining characteristic." This is not to say that the complex pattern illustrated in the satisfaction of each member is the same, that the members are identical. In a perspectival universe, pure identity is impossible. The defining characteristic of a society partially shapes the satisfactions of its members, gives them certain general characteristics in common, mediates and canalizes their subjective diversity. An entity emerging in a social environment arises out of data which already exhibit some degree of shared order and which thus are susceptible to more complex integrations than unordered data.[19] In a social context, the communality of the shared form mediates the inhibitions and incompatibilities in the various elements of the data, enabling them to be synthesized as relevant contrasts. Without communality, conflicting elements (disorder) would have to be prehended negatively or at best integrated in trivial ways, thus limiting the complexity achievable in the satisfaction. Since the depth and value of a satisfaction are directly proportionate to the aesthetic character of its complexity, a social environment is essential for the emergence of high-grade occasions, i.e., occasions whose experience as "feeler" is intense and whose superjection adds novel value to the universe.

Since the defining characteristic of a society is exemplified in each of its members, a concrescent occasion inherits it as an element to be incorporated in its own definiteness and superjected to future occasions.

> Thus a set of entities is a society (i) in virtue of a "defining characteristic" shared by its members, and (ii) in virtue of the presence of the defining characteristic being due to the environment provided by the society itself.[20]

The defining characteristic and the social "laws" flowing from it do not add any new formal elements to the society in question;

nor are they imposed on the society by some outside agency. They arise in a nexus as a result of already present similarities among the original members and guarantee the reproduction of analogous similarities among future members. Thus a metaphysical "socialization" ensures the propagation of the defining characteristic and hence the endurance of the society.

This endurance has temporal limits, however. Just as there are no "simply located particles" in the Whiteheadian cosmology, things requiring nothing outside themselves in order to exist, so also there are no "simply located" societies capable of providing all that is necessary for the survival of their members. As Whitehead figuratively expresses it, a society, particularly a living society, requires food:[21] i.e., it is dependent on the presence of more general characteristics in the wider environment, aspects important for the maintenance of the more specialized characteristics whereby it defines itself.[22] Sufficient change in this wider environment leads to the collapse of the included societies. Their defining characteristic sinks into irrelevance for the included members. The endurance of societies is, therefore, epochal in character—they arise, flourish, and decay.

This description of society in its most general sense is strictly applicable only to phenomena such as a physical field in empty space. A more specialized interpretation is necessary when the term is to be applied to more mundane objects, an interpretation which does not abrogate the fundamental characteristics of society but adds other limiting conditions. The first step beyond the social nature of the intermittent "flashes" of existence which constitute a field is toward what Whitehead calls "personal order." The order manifested by a society is deemed personal when the members are arranged by a linear or serial propagation of the defining characteristic, such that the inheritance relations are not symmetrical.[23] The career of an electron in time manifests such order, as does the conscious life of a man. Each episodic occasion in a personal order bears a social relation to past occasions in the same thread. It arises out of its own history in a peculiarly intimate way and is provoked by that history to reiterate the personal defining characteristic in the present. Such threads of personal order take the place of what ordinary language would call particles or wave trains.

The enduring objects of our everyday experience are social

organizations of many strands of such personal threads: in Whitehead's language, "corpuscular Societies." On the primitive level, they manifest no social order more complex than the "horizontal" order binding the threads together. Higher-grade enduring objects are characterized by an increase in "vertical" social structure in the sense that the society represents the patterned togetherness of sub-societies which themselves may be composed of sub-societies, etc. Such a structured society provides a highly favorable environment for members arising within the included sub-societies and personal threads. The data[24] out of which such an individual creates its perspective are already rich in shared order;[25] therefore the resultant unity and stability of the enduring object is enhanced. Figuratively speaking, each individual inherits and ratifies its position and function in the complex whole and ensures the propagation of the pattern defining the whole.

Such "reactionary" societies have high survival value because of this massive patterning of inheritance, but at the same time they inhibit the personal, originative inwardness of their members. "An enduring entity binds any one of its occasions to the line of its ancestry." [26] The immediacy or subjectivity of these members is limited to a mere reiterated synthesis of the past in the present. Furthermore, given the dominance of inheritance from the past, a structured society is unable to initiate adaptive responses to significant changes in the larger environment it inhabits. It copes with minor changes by blocking them out, by "ignoring" them while they carry on their subtle erosive activity. Major changes overwhelm the society and bring about its extinction. The inorganic world thus wears a mask of permanence covering its gradual entropy. The price of the mask is paid in the triviality of the lives of its members.

Such a notion cannot be the social paradigm in a philosophy in which creativity, novelty, and intensity play so important a role as they do for Whitehead.[27] The notion of life supplies what is lacking in the inorganic description. The living occasion is characterized by its escape from inheritance. "Life is a bid for freedom" [28]—freedom from efficient causality, from the pressure of the past, from the necessity of repeating old solutions in the face of new problems; freedom for reaction dictated by the present not the past, for the capture of intensity, originality, and the clutch at vivid immediacy.²⁹ Life cannot be social, for society binds the present to the past.

The anti-social character of a living occasion, its independence of inheritance, though the key to intensity, is at the same time problematic with respect to the value of the satisfaction achieved. Value is a trivalent term for Whitehead:

> Everything has some value for itself, for others, and for the whole. . . . No unit can separate itself from the others, and from the whole. And yet each unit exists in its own right. It upholds value-intensity for itself, and this involves sharing value-intensity with the universe.³⁰

The absolute "for-itself-ness" of an isolated living occasion would be superjected to the universe as anarchic disorder, inhibiting the attainment of value on the part of the others. Furthermore, an isolated living occasion could not achieve value-intensity even for itself because of its independence of previously achieved order in the environment.³¹ This is to say, therefore, that an isolated living occasion would negate the interfusion of nature and be an exception in the metaphysics of organism. If life is to be possible, if a living occasion is to arise, it must arise in a social context. Non-social itself, it needs the environment of a structured society to provide an orderly world for it to react originatively to, and an ordered world to assimilate its novel contributions. "Life lurks in the interstices of each living cell, and in the interstices of the brain," ³² sheltered in the bodily environment, receiving as its data the patterning of the external environment produced by the sub-societies of the body, reacting originatively to those data, and thus contributing to the body its capacity to react adaptively to environmental change. It is therefore capable of being sensitive to the past without being bound to the past, and of giving to the body a behavioral flexibility not possible for a body which does not harbor living occasions.

> An electron within a living body is different from an electron outside it, by reason of the plan of body. The electron blindly runs either within or without the body; but it runs within the body in accordance with its character within the body; that is to say, in accordance with the general plan of the body, and this plan includes the mental state.³³

The pinnacle of living occasions is reached, and the dichotomy between life and society is overcome, when a series of living occasions develops a thread of continuity which is perpetuated through the serial inheritance of a defining characteristic or "personality." In this way, the novelty of each episodic occasion in the thread is canalized and intensified through the inheritance of the character without being inhibited by it, in much the same way as a painter's creative genius is channeled in his successive works by the elusive phenomenon known as his "style." Intensity and creativity are mated with historic continuity, originality with inheritance.

In the context of the foregoing encapsulation of Whitehead's metaphysical sociology, a further methodological consideration must be introduced to enable an application of the speculative categories to human society to avoid the pitfalls of Misplaced Concreteness. There are two types of analysis according to which an actual occasion can be described: the genetic and morphological modes.[34] The former takes as its primary datum the given out of which an occasion arises, and traces the process whereby the public past is woven together into a moment of privacy. It is an analysis of the subjectification of the occasion, yielding the genetic sequence of feelings or prehensions by which the subjective aim realizes itself in the satisfaction, and witnessing the efficient causality of the environment being overwhelmed by the final causality of the emergent occasion. On the other hand, morphological or coordinate division is an analysis of the superject, of the concrete drop of space–time which the concrescence has produced. It is, further, an analysis which proceeds by eliminating the private, immediate unity and internal finality of the subject, and, by examining only its public or superjective career, the ways in which the satisfied occasion functions as efficient cause of futures. Neither of these modes of analysis is complete in itself; each requires the other to correct the partiality resultant from its viewpoint. Just as it is impossible to isolate process and outcome, subject and superject, without falling into Misplaced Concreteness, so neither mode of analysis is independent of the other. To exclude coordinate analysis is to have refused acknowledgment to the public character of the world of fact and to have fallen into the crudest sorts of subjectivism and animism, in which "science is the daydream of an individual without any public import," [35] and nature operates solely by private intentions and purposes. When, on the other hand, co-ordinate analysis is taken as the total description of nature, the world is reduced to a qualityless, characterless machine in which efficient causality is publicly transferred from one, simple, located, vacuous particle to another *ad infinitum* without any private assimilation, and the scientific mechanism Whitehead delineated in the opening chapters of *Science and the Modern World* rules supreme.

The point at issue here is the classical matter–mind problem, only now translated into methodological terms. Coordinate division, as the technique characteristic of the scientist, concentrates on the public adventures of matter in metric space–time, and its analyses achieve their quasi-exactitude from the fact that they do not take into account the private, "subjective" reactions of whatever extended bodies are their focus of concern. The phenomenologist, the psychoanalyst, the humanistic psychologist, and others who are concerned more with the interiority of the reactants, make use of genetic analysis. Only this type of analysis can reveal the function "such non-physical things as purposes, deliberations, plans, decisions, theories, tensions, and values can play . . . in bringing about changes in the physical world." [36]

It is important to note that Whitehead makes the matter–mind dichotomy an element of all reality, not merely of those bodies normally considered as possessing mentality. Any actual occasion has both physical and conceptual feelings, which is to say that in its concrescence it grasps not only facts (past efficiencies) but the forms (patterns, purposes, qualities, etc.) through which the publicity of the past can be synthesized into a moment of private enjoyment. The conceptual feelings through which the forms enter a concrescence are conscious only under severely limited conditions such as those exemplified in the higher animals—therefore awareness is not to be considered a prime characteristic of mentality; yet, they are essentially different from purely physical feelings in that their objects are different. The problem faced by every concrescence is the welding together of both sorts of feelings into a private unity. In low-grade occasions, the role mentality has to play is trivial—hence the physicist can legitimately ignore the privacy of particles; whereas in high-grade occasions, conceptual feelings become important and cannot be eliminated from an account of the behavior of an occasion without rendering that account a mere half-truth. However, to fail to recognize the role which environmental efficiency plays in the formative process of high-grade occasions is likewise to fall victim to half-truth. When analyzing the arising of human individuals in human society, it is therefore critical to give equal attention to mentality and efficiency, to genetic and coordinate division, thereby avoiding extremist theories which reduce either pole to the other by exalting either mode of analysis at the expense of the other.

II. *Beyond Freedom and Dignity*:
THE FALLACY OF PARTIALITY

In his construction of a science of human behavior, B. F. Skinner sees the dichtomy between methodologies in other terms—terms unfortunate for the development of a complete view of individual–societal relations. He calls "pre-scientific" the attitude which explains human behavior by appealing to internal and hence unobservable sources, and he notes:

> Physics did not advance by looking more closely at the jubilance of a falling body, or biology by looking at the nature of vital spirits, and we do not need to try to discover what personalities, states of mind, feelings, traits of character, plans, purposes, intentions, or the other perquisites of autonomous man really are in order to get on with a scientific analysis of behavior.[37]

For Skinner, this scientific analysis looks to the environment for explanations; not to an environment which crudely compels certain sorts of behavior, but to an environment in which the consequences of modes of behavior reinforce the repetition or avoidance of those modes in the future. He is not seeking to construct a neo-Pavlovianism of crude s-r conditioning; rather he looks to the subtle interaction of individual and environment through time, and he analyzes what others would call learning or habit-formation. His expressed aim is the construction of a technology of operant behavior on the presupposition that a person's behavior is determined by a genetic endowment traceable to the evolutionary history of the species and by the environmental circumstances to which as an individual he has been exposed.[38]

What he has realized is what Whitehead would certainly applaud: namely, that individuals arise out of a social and non-social environment and inherit their defining characteristic (or character) from that environment. Of course Skinner would insist that "character" be replaced by "repertoire of behavior," but the two terms are not so drastically opposed as he would believe. Skinner's straw man[39]—the autonomous man who inhabits the literature of freedom—derives his "in-himself-ness" from an implicit substance-metaphysics which interprets the person as some sort of supposit enduring through time, and thereby providing the unity of his various behavioral manifestations. In a process metaphysics, no such view is tenable. The "ghost in the machine" is replaced by a pattern, derived originally from the environment, which undergoes modification as a result of interaction with a changing environment, and is inherited from occasion to occasion of a person's existence, canalizing his behavior into the unity of a lifestyle. In Skinner's view,

a self is a repertoire of behavior appropriate to a given set of contingencies. . . . The identity conferred upon a self arises from the contingencies responsible for the behavior. . . . The picture which emerges from a scientific analysis is not of a body with a person inside, but of a body which *is* a person in the sense that it displays a complex repertoire of behavior.[40]

For both Whitehead and Skinner, therefore, character or repertoire of behavior, the factor providing the unity of personal life, is ultimately a function of the environment, taking environment in the broad sense to include the historic past of the person, the past of the species, and the historic social and non-social context out of which he arises and to which he responds.

From the cultural environment, the individual absorbs the "values" and "ideas" [41] which give this character its broad delineation. The culture is the pattern of social customs which provides the most general form of order in a human environment, an order adapted to the contingencies in the geographical and historical environment, and, hence, idiosyncratic. The culture is assimilated by each individual in the society through a series of negative and positive reinforcements in childhood, and transmitted by him to future generations. Cultures arise to shelter individuals by providing inherited responses to environmental contingencies, thus promoting the survival both of the individuals and of the behavior patterns.[42] In Whiteheadian language, cultures originate out of the analogous similarities in the objectifications of members of a nexus. In a human society, a person is objectified in his behavior (his public career): behavior which is an originative response to environmental change. The success of the response becomes part of the data for other members of the group. In imitating the response, they thus provide the inherited similarities which distinguish a society from a mere nexus. What is inherited is precisely what is the common element in the objectifications of the members: the shared behavior pattern, the generalized repertoire.

Despite similarities which structure the "long view" of both theories, they diverge in their interpretation of these basic facts. It is unfortunate that Skinner does not make an adequate distinction between behavior and behavior pattern, for had he done so, he might have avoided the conclusions which drove him to deny any reality to inner man. Although he uses the language of "repertoire," it is the behavior itself he considers, not its patterning. Behavior is mere efficient causality, be it the behavior of a molecule or of a man. It is sheer, brute, compulsive fact. As such, it is an abstraction with no more concrete reality than the "f" in $f = ma$. In the concrete, "f" is always some *kind* of force: mechanical, electro-magnetic, etc., and behavior is some *kind* of behavior. Both are indeed efficiencies, but *patterned* efficiencies, illustrating the inextricable togetherness of fact and form in concrete reality and demanding for Whitehead the two-sided conception of experience embodied in the terms "physical" and "conceptual" prehension. Any occasion has a mental side[43] through which the patterns of its environment are grasped. Granted: this "grasping" need not be conscious; it is nonetheless the grasp of something of the nature of an idea. Whitehead sees mentality as pervading the universe, embodied in all occasions from the crudest to the most sophisticated. What differentiates an inorganic occasion from an organic or living one is not mentality but the manner in which environmental patterns are woven together to form the patterned satisfaction. The inorganic occasion merely repeats the inherited pattern in its own definiteness —it transmits the force across itself to the future. A living occasion is not so bound to the patterns in its past. If it were, no new patterns could ever appear—evolution would be a logical impossibility.

Transposed to the personal and cultural level, this is to say that Skinner's theory may provide an account for the survival of a behavioral repertoire or of a culture, but not for its evolution. He likens the emergence of new practices to genetic mutations, but continually sidesteps further questions,[44] or speaks vaguely of "accidents"[45] and "conditioned reinforcers."[46] Whitehead is far more explicit in his account of the emergence of novel behavior. When confronted with an environmental change detrimental to the organism, a living occasion solves the problem

> by an *initiative*[47] in conceptual prehensions, i.e., in appetition. The purpose of this initiative is to receive the novel elements of the environment into explicit feelings with such subjective forms as conciliate them with the complex experiences proper to members of the structured society. Thus in each concrescent occasion its subjective aim originates novelty to match the novelty of the environment. In the case of the higher organisms, this conceptual initiative amounts to *thinking* about the diverse experiences.[48]

On the macro-social level, this would imply that the masses in a culture tend by necessity to be conservative or reactionary; but that certain creative members[49] can envision non-traditional solutions to environmental problems. These solutions, if compatible with the traditional cultural pattern, are integrated with it and themselves become tradition. The creative solution does not come *ex nihilo*; nor is its novelty absolute and unconditioned. It must be both culturally consistent and historically relevant if it is not to fall within the realm of pathology.[50] Furthermore, the creatively initiated response must "work"—the novel behavior must be reinforced by environmental feedback—if it is to become traditional rather than idiosyncratic. Thus initiative is not the radically independent phenomenon Skinner describes and then demonstrates to be impossible. It is circumscribed by physical, environmental, historical, and cultural conditions which channel it and render it efficacious. It is solicited and given its general shape by facts in the past environment; it is verified or falsified by facts in the future environment. But between these poles of efficient causality lies a moment of creative, final causality. It is this moment, not moments of choice, which exemplifies personal autonomy, human freedom. The free man is not the man *free from* environmental control, for in the philosophy of organism, the individual *is* the environment as structured into a unique perspective; nor is he the man *free to* act randomly upon the environment. The free man is the artist of life who can transcend the necessity of reiterating the patterns which shape him and his environment and initiate relevant new patterns. He is the man *free for* conditioned novelty.

It is impossible to interpret this notion within the framework of a coordinate analysis, as Skinner attempts to do, for internality and final causality do not appear as elements of facts. They emerge only in analyses of process. What the behavioral scientist observes with methodological correctness are the chains of interaction between individual and environment whereby habits are strengthened or weakened; what he describes are the modalities of control which the social and non-social environment exercises in the formation of individuals. To maintain a naïve theory of autonomous man in the light of such data is to be both metaphysically simplistic and scientifically blind. But to deny any sort of autonomy to man on the same grounds is to be equally blind to an important aspect of experience—that aspect comprising the "purposes, plans, deliberations, tensions, and values" of which Popper speaks.[51] "An actual entity is a process, and is not describable in terms of the morphology of a 'stuff.' "[52]

> However far the sphere of efficient causality be pushed in the determination of components of a concrescence, . . . beyond the determination of these components there always remains the final reaction of the self-creative unity of the universe.[53]

That ideas, emotions, appreciations, and purposes have any causal relation to behavior is precisely what Skinner denies. Reversing more than 2500 years of an attitude which he sees as a reduction of behavior to the status of a by-product of mental activity,[54] he asserts the entire range of mental life to be a mere by-product of behavior.[55] He thus denies any effective status to internal "feelings," arguing that "we do not feel the things which have been invented to explain behavior",[56] we feel the behavior and certain physical states of the organism (contingencies in the "inner" environment which are not different in kind from those in the outer environment).[57] In a very curious manner, he separates feelings from both behavior and inner contingencies, and leaves them floating in thin air. He refuses to attribute them to his banished homunculus and yet is unable to give a coherent account of them. For example, he states:

> What a person *feels* when he feels himself wanting something depends on the circumstances. Food is reinforcing only in a state of deprivation, and a person who wants something to eat may feel part of that state—for example, hunger pangs.[58]

And in another place,

> What we attribute to an object when we call it red, rough, or sweet is in part a condition of our own body, resulting . . . from recent stimulation.[59]

Yet the physiological condition present in a hungry stomach or a red-seeing eye is not the same as the *feeling* of hunger or the *awareness* of red. Such conditions are public and observable; feelings are not. To say that feelings are by-products of bodily states and thereby unimportant is to explain away what is unexplainable within the limits of the methodology.

Skinner's conception of the relation between feelings and reinforcers is likewise unclear. He declares that "there is no important causal connection between the reinforcing effect of a stimulus and the feelings to which it gives rise";[60] that "stimuli are reinforcing and produce conditions which are felt as good for a single reason, to be found in an evolutionary history." [61] If "the important thing is not the feeling but thing felt," [62] can it be said that an environmental stimulus could function as a reinforcer if it were not felt-as-good? He certainly takes a contrary position in his discussion of value:

> When we say that a value judgment is a matter not of fact but
> of how someone feels about a fact, we are simply distinguish-
> ing between a thing and its reinforcing effect. . . . To make a
> value judgment by calling something good or bad is to classify
> it in terms of its reinforcing effects.[63]

Yet the reinforcing effect is to him the resultant physiological
change, not the feeling. The feeling cannot even be ascribed to
the agency of the reinforcement. Of the three elements involved
in his analysis—reinforcers, reinforcing effects, and feelings-of-
reinforcement—he continually muddies the relation between the
last two. When he speaks of reinforcement as the cause of behavior, it is clearly reinforcement consciously felt; yet when he
speaks of conscious feelings, he maintains that they are unimportant, mere by-products.

Generalizing from this position, he attributes the arising of
awareness to the influence of external social contingencies.

> The verbal community specializes in self-descriptive contin-
> gencies. It asks such questions as: What did you do yesterday?
> What are you doing now? What will you do tomorrow? Why
> did you do that? Do you really want to do that? How do you
> feel about that? The answers help people to adjust to each
> other effectively. And it is because such questions are asked
> that a person responds to himself and his behavior in the spe-
> cial way called knowing or being aware. Without the help of
> a verbal community all behavior would be unconscious. Con-
> sciousness is a social product. It is not only *not* the special field
> of autonomous man, it is not within the range of a solitary
> man.[64]

Is this to say that a solitary or feral man would not *feel* hunger
or pain or anger, or merely that he could not render more precise
or describe the content of his awareness? In the absence of a
verbal community, is the world "inside the skin" reducible to
the physiological activities which precede behavior? Is consciousness merely an epiphenomenon of language?

Skinner passes off such questions to the physiological sciences,
with the hope that they will "stop looking for the physiological
correlates of mental events," leave aside questions of "personalities, ideas, feelings, impulses, thoughts or purposes" which their

methodologies are not "designed to detect or measure," and get on with their proper business of explaining "why behavior is indeed related to the antecedent events of which it can be shown to be a function." [65] Once these relations have been clarified, he believes that the specter of mind can be banished completely. Would that the ghost could be exorcised from the machine so readily! Perhaps the more appropriate exclamation is, "Would that metaphysics were so easy to do!"

It has often been said in criticism of Skinner that he has no metaphysics. This may be partly true, for he never gives his analyses the sort of unity and coherence which appear when a scientific position is grounded in an explicit metaphysics. However, it can be argued that there is a definite though implicit metaphysics undergirding the view of man which he creates and then rejects, a metaphysics already characterized above as substance-oriented. Skinner's attitude toward mind reveals further that he understands classical mind–body speculation in a crudely Cartesian manner. Note the alternatives he sets up with respect to mind and man: consciousness is the result of either an external agency or an internal agent; feelings are either irrelevant by-products of behavior or its cause; either human behavior is controlled adversely or aversely by the environment or it is radically autonomous;[66] man is either a complex repertoire of behavior or "a body with a person inside." [67] The only metaphysical alternatives he sees are his own unelaborated and uncriticized monism or a dualism of the naïvist sort—similar to a high school girl's understanding of Descartes. The dualism radically separates mind and matter, finality and efficiency, freedom and determinism, consciousness and action, quality and quantity, but cannot come up with a pineal body to account for the dominance of the first in each pair over the second. Skinner gratuitously assumes that the rejection of this straw homunculus, a rejection necessitated by the array of scientific evidence he marshals against it, leaves his theory as the only viable alternative. Is it viable, however? And is it the only other option?

Unfortunately, the metaphysical presuppositions of the theory he proposes are as incoherent as the dualism he rejects. In separating mentality from behavior, his exorcism has backfired. He has merely created a new ghost in the machine, this time a genuine specter—a shadowy illusion haunting the repertoire of behavior but unable to affect it. In denying finality he has created the sheriff without a court which Peirce attacked, a cause whose effect may be *post hoc* but not *propter hoc*.[68] Furthermore, his interpretation of freedom as the absence of control, and his subsequent attempts to reject such a notion of freedom, leave him entangled in what is merely a more subtle form of crude environmentalism. He believes that he has eluded Pavlovianism by recognizing that the human environment is increasingly manmade; hence, the control which environment exercises over man is in fact human control. "Man as we know him, for better or for worse, is what man has made of man." [69] He proposes the exhilarating vision of man deliberately designing cultures, consciously engineering behavior,[70] creating a paradise to make himself a saint.[71] But with creative mind out of the picture, with ideas, abstractions, generalizations, plans, and purposes merely unimportant by-products of behavior, which itself is a function of environmental contingencies of reinforcement, what is to initiate and reinforce new behavior in an old environment? Skinner argues that

> the culture promotes thinking by constructing special contingencies. It teaches a person to make fine discriminations by making differential reinforcement more precise. It teaches techniques to be used in solving problems. It provides rules which make it unnecessary to be exposed to the contingencies from which the rules are derived, and it provides rules for finding rules.[72]

However, this "promoting," "teaching," and "providing" are elements in the behavior of individuals and hence shaped by the cultural past. The modes of thinking reinforced in such an environment would be explicative, not ampliative, yielding merely variants of traditional solutions and not new answers. Pavlov has not been buried too deeply; when the excess verbiage has been cut away, the environment still stimulates and man responds. By misconstruing and then denying creative mentality, Skinner is metaphysically driven to attribute novelty to accident,[73] to random factors in the non-social or social environment.

In a word, Skinnerian environmentalism may work as behavioral science because of the necessity for any science to restrict itself to coordinate analysis of the observable, thereby deliberately excluding from its purview the subjectivity of its objects, but it does not work as a metaphysics. A repertoire of behavior inhabited by a nebulous and ineffective consciousness is as incoherent a theoretical description of man as is a body with a person inside. Skinnerian behaviorism is a half-truth.

III. MENTALITY AND BEHAVIOR: A WHITEHEADIAN RESPONSE

The same phenomena which Skinner must treat as non-existent or irrelevant can be handled in a genetic analysis without falling into a crude dualism. Furthermore, elements in Skinner's theory which seem to have a shaky basis can be placed on a firmer foundation. Whitehead's model of a concrescence can account for the full range of environmental and genetic influence on a person without at the same time trivializing the role of emotion, consciousness, purpose, and creative freedom.

The external and internal environment provide the given, the raw materials out of which the conscious monad [74] creates itself. "Each task of creation is a social effort, employing the whole universe." [75] The datum is a public and highly complex integration of the efficiency of the personal, racial, social, and non-social past—of the totality of the inner and outer worlds.[76] The concrescence of the conscious monad is a further and private integration of this datum.[77]

The initial stage of reception and conformation—the stage in which the multiplicity of the universe is reduced to unity privately assimilable—is the phase in the concrescence which is most germane to a critique of Skinner, for it is here that privacy and autonomy enter the picture, not in later stages characterized by consciousness. Whitehead maintains that "consciousness presupposes experience, and not experience consciousness. . . . [An actual entity's] experience is its complete formal constitution, including its consciousness, if any." [78] The initial data of any concrescence are the objectified satisfactions of the immediately past world, which for the conscious monad is the bodily society. The inhibitions and incompatibilities remaining in the data must be simplified and overcome if a concrescent unity of any degree of intensity is to be attained. This simplification is achieved through a process whereby compatible aspects in the satisfactions of the manifold are positively prehended, and the rest dismissed in negative prehensions. Thus, a single element in the definiteness of each past bodily occasion—one of its many feelings—is taken to stand for the total complex of feeling which is its satisfaction.[79] What remains as a result of this process of selection is the unity of sympathetic feelings; the data have become a datum.

However, such a process is possible only if the subject has some antecedent "idea of itself" to norm the selections and eliminations.

> The feelings *aim at* their subject. . . . An actual entity feels as it does feel in order to be the actual entity which it is. . . . An actuality is self-realizing. . . . The attainment of a peculiar definiteness is the final cause which animates a particular process.[80]

This implies, therefore, that a concrescence originates out of *both* the efficiency of the environment *and* the finality of the subject. Whitehead, in contradistinction to Skinner, sees these two modes of causal functioning as mutually interwoven.[81]

The subjective aim of the occasion, its "idea of itself" which is final cause of the process, is not derived from within an autonomous subject,[82] but from the environment. Whitehead sees each Actual World as, figuratively speaking, surrounded by a halo of relevant patterns according to which it could be integrated,[83] the multiplicity of these patterns being a function of the antecedent order in the Actual World in question. Furthermore, these patterns are graded in relevance with respect to the environment, some capable of norming more complex and novel integrations than others. One of these environmentally suggested possibles becomes the initial aim of the subject, norming its process of self-realization.

> This doctrine of the inherence of the subject in the process of its production requires that in the primary phase of the subjective process there be a conceptual feeling of subjective aim: the physical and other feelings originate as steps toward realizing this conceptual aim through their treatment of initial data.[84]

To explain the manner in which one out of the manifold of relevant possibilities is felt as the initial aim, it is necessary to probe deeper into the Whiteheadian conception of mentality, for he is taking the position that any process originates through conceptual functioning. Mentality, not to be confused with either consciousness or thought, is synonymous with appetition—the tendency toward the realization of a form.

> Appetition is immediate matter of fact including in itself a principle of unrest, involving realization of what is not and may be.[85]

A conceptual feeling is not, therefore, a bland receptivity of forms in the environment; nor is form itself to be considered as pure passivity waiting to be appropriated. Both have about them all the unrest latent in the Platonic *eros*; a form "lures" entities to incorporate it in their definiteness; mentality is the appetitive grasp of and response to that lure. The goal of both is the "capture of intensity," [86] of private, vivid, novel immediacy in the satisfaction;[87] in a word, the creation of a value[88] which will lure future processes to embody it.[89] This insistent interplay of lures and appetites is the creativity of the universe.

In such a context, the role played by the initial aim of a concrescence becomes clearer. Of the manifold of possible ways in which a given Actual World could be unified into a perspective, the one which will promote the greatest intensity in the satisfaction becomes the lure or final cause of the process.[90] Note how readily this could be translated into Skinnerian terms. The intensity of a satisfaction, the way it "feels," is the feeling-of-reinforcement;[91] the complexity of the satisfaction, of which intensity is a function, is the final synthesis of the condition-of-reinforcement in the body. Skinner, however, sees the reinforcement as a mechanical product of environmental agency. For Whitehead, it is a subjective creation in response to an environmental lure. It cannot even be said that the lure as originally grasped and the lure as finally concretized in the shape of the satisfaction are identical, for this would reduce autonomy to responsiveness, and human subjectivity would become a mere private reiteration of the environment.

The initial aim may be provided by, and be relevant to, the

environment,[92] but the emergent perspective modifies it, rendering it uniquely personal. The aim as originally felt is partly vague and indeterminate—it suggests a "species" of realization, not the fully determinate concreteness of the satisfaction. It becomes determinate through the decisions of the concrescent occasion; it is fleshed out, personalized, simplified, through the adjustments of emphasis and modifications introduced by the subject in its response to the particularities of the environment.

> As soon as individual experience is not negligible, the autonomy of the subject in the modification of its initial subjective aim must be taken into account.[93]

Under the presiding unity of the aim, each physical feeling of the efficiency of the environment, each conceptual feeling of environmentally realized forms, each selection, each elimination, each subsequent integration of the initial given, each adjustment of emphasis, is clothed with a subjective form[94] which both makes the feeling private and adds to the emergent definiteness of the aim. The initial aim stands to the fully realized satisfaction as "human being" stands to "Socrates." Socrates embodies humanity, but in a uniquely personal Socratic manner. His feeling-of-being-Socrates is the feeling-of-being-human made private through the integration of his various personal responses to the Socratic environment.

With the notion of subjective form, emotion enters the model of self-realization which Whitehead proposes.[95] Unlike Skinner, who treats emotions as subjective, irrelevant, inexplicable byproducts of environmental influence, Whitehead sees them as inextricable aspects of the process of feeling.[96] They do not qualify a physical or conceptual feeling in an accidental manner; they *are* the way the feeling feels,[97] the way the subject subjectivizes the data.[98] Thus Whitehead can integrate emotion into the self-realization of a subject without making it either a cause or a side effect of behavior. The same can be said of perception, thought, and conscious purpose in high-grade occasions. They are the subjective form of feelings which arise in later phases of a concrescence, various ways in which "objectivity is absorbed into subjectivity." [99] Through them, "the 'scalar' form overwhelms the original 'vector' form. . . . The vector form,[100] is not lost, but is submerged as the foundation of the scalar[101] superstructure." [102] Conscious phenomena are not independent of experience, as Skinner maintains, but are criticisms, simplifications, and integrations of earlier phases of experience, i.e., of more primitive feelings. Consciousness is "the culmination of the universe and not a stage-play about it." [103]

What differentiates these later feelings from the more primitive, conformal feelings is the emergence of more and more novelty.[104] A simple physical feeling originates as tied to the datum. It merely repeats the objectified feeling of the datum from its perspective, reiterating the subjective form of the feeling felt.[105] In subsequent phases, however, the subject can transcend the possibilities actualized in the data and grasp novel possibilities relevant to, but not actualized in, the data. With such "propositional feelings," the subject approaches what ordinary language calls mentality—it can entertain novel objectives for itself and be lured to realize them in its determinateness. Efficiency is fully translated into finality; freedom for self-creativity overwhelms environmental determinism.

When consciousness arises in the presence of adequately structured data, it illumines primarily the phase in which it arises; hence it does not present the data in their concreteness. What it clearly and distinctly represents is an abstraction several steps removed from the data and not the data as immediately felt. At the same time, however, it dimly illumines the earlier phases of the concrescence, the emotions, valuations, and purposes which characterize the initial receptive and appreciative feelings.

Notice how this interpretation clarifies still further the relation between a reinforcement and the feeling-of-reinforcement. On the preconscious level, the efficiency of the reinforcer[106] was prehended by the emerging monad with the subjective forms of adversion—as conducive to the realization of its subjective aim at intensity—and hence "appreciated," unconsciously valued as good. This emotional feeling is raised to dim consciousness in the conscious monad's abstract display of its Actual World.[107] It is not, therefore, a subsequent by-product of the reinforcement, but *is* the way the bodily condition is appropriated by the subject.

In a similar fashion, behavior, the concrete way in which the conscious monad objectifies itself for the future, is neither consciously nor emotionally produced. To assert either alternative as the *cause* of behavior is to fall into Misplaced Concreteness, since emotion and consciousness are elements in the larger reality of the self-creative process which behavior climaxed. They are adverbial modifiers of behavior, not autonomous causes. Only the subject itself—that quantum of process stretched between initial data and terminal satisfaction—is autonomous; and that subject is the totality of reality grown together to constitute a novel addition to itself.

Skinner's ultimate misconception, the concealed dualistic hypothesis which pervades even the monistic metaphysics he implicitly assumes, is the bifurcation of subject and environment, individual and society. For Whitehead, no entity is an island isolated from the social ocean surrounding it. He rejects the classical dichotomy between individual and environment and views the individual as a perspectival culmination of the environment, without at the same time reducing either pole to the other. Entities arise from a common past, contribute their novelty to a common future; but in their concrescent process they suffer alone in causal independence of their contemporaries. This is the meaning of autonomy for Whitehead. The culmination of the universe takes place in a self-creative moment of privacy, issuing from an Actual World made unique by the perspectival eliminations, governed by ideals made personal in the process, and producing a novel drop of immediate self-enjoyment. Autonomy is not equivalent to independence, for independence is always independence *from* some other thing.

Thus, any sociology which isolates man from society either to assert or to deny his dependence on it is doubly guilty of the Simple Location Fallacy. It is not simply the case that human experience is impossible outside of a social, cultural environment, for a subtle dualism can still infect such an interpretation. Rather, the conscious monad is the final node of a manifold of integrations of that environment. As two converging lines define a space which culminates in a unique point, so society effects individuals. It is perfectly legitimate, therefore, to speak of the inherence of a culture in the character of an individual, of culturally conditioned values, of the role of language in structuring human consciousness, etc., so long as human experience is seen as the "final reaction of the self-creative unity of the universe." [108] "Each creative act is the universe incarnating itself as one." [109] Each incarnation lures the universe onward to further creative acts, adding a new condition to be absorbed in future process. Man is in society, of society, and for society; society is in man, of man, and for man. Each achieves value, novelty, and intensity through the other. As opposed elements, they "stand to each other in mutual requirement," [110] subjectivity emerging from objectivity, objectivity from subjectivity. Privacy and publicity, finality and efficiency, mentality and materiality, freedom and necessity, are paired opposites by reason of which man and society are involved in a never-ending process of self-transcendence. "All the 'opposites' are elements in the nature of things, and are incorrigibly there." [111] They are inescapable elements in the data of experience; they clamor for equal rank in any interpretation of experience. *In fine*, they express

the final metaphysical truth that appetitive vision and physical enjoyment have equal claim to priority in creation.[112]

NOTES

1. In this case, a group of actual occasions: "the final real things of which the world is made up, . . . drops of experience, complex and interdependent." Alfred North Whitehead, *Process and Reality* (New York: Harper Torchbooks, 1960), p. 23. Hereafter, PR.

2. Such a fact of togetherness among occasions is termed a nexus, PR, p. 30.

3. See PR, pp. 5-6.

4. PR, p. 4.

5. PR, p. 7.

6. PR, p. 13.

7. *Ibid.*

8. *Ibid.*

9. B. F. Skinner, *Walden II* (New York: Macmillan Paperbacks, 1962), p. 273

10. Prehended.

11. Positive prehension.

12. The "how" a fact is grasped—its emotive valuation, etc.

13. "'Concrescence' is the name for the process in which the universe of many things acquires an individual unity in a determinate relation of

each item of the 'many' to its subordination in the constitution of the novel 'one.' " PR, p. 321.

14. Ideal aimed at in the concrescence, the subject's "idea of itself" which governs the process of self-realization.

15. Called objectifications.

16. PR, p. 136.

17. "The many become one, and are increased by one." PR, p. 32.

18. PR, p. 138.

19. The importance of an aesthetic sort of complexity in the satisfaction will become relevant in later discussions of the private aspect of a concrescence. For the purposes of this part of the exposition, it is necessary to provide only the metaphysical basis for the possibility of complexity.

20. PR, p. 137.

21. PR, p. 160.

22. E.g., the social characteristics and laws which determine an atom to be iron presuppose the more general characters and laws which govern the electronic and protonic societies within it.

23. E.g., in a personal order constituted by occasions A, B, and C, B inherits from A, C inherits from B and A, but neither A nor B inherits from C.

24. Or Actual World.

25. The patterns inherited from its personal past, the past of its subsociety and the other included sub-societies, and from the environing structured society.

26. PR, p. 150.

27. The concrescence of any occasion is its grasp at novel immediacy —its self-determination. Its satisfaction is in part determined and limited by the efficient causality of the past, but the occasion functions with respect to its own determinacy under the final causality of the subjective aim. A concrescence is a more or less purposive activity whose goal is intensity of experience produced by the realization of patterned novelty.

28. PR, p. 159.

29. PR, p. 160.

30. Alfred North Whitehead, *Modes of Thought* (New York: Capricorn, 1958), p. 151.

31. It would have to "start from scratch," so to speak, in ordering its data.

32. PR, p. 161.

33. Alfred North Whitehead, *Science and the Modern World* (New York: Free Press, 1967), p. 79.

34. Also termed genetic and coordinate division.

35. PR, p. 508.

36. Karl R. Popper, *Of Clouds and Clocks* (St. Louis: Washington University, 1966), p. 15.

37. B. F. Skinner, *Beyond Freedom and Dignity* (New York: Bantam, 1972), pp. 12-13. Hereafter, BFD.

38. BFD, p. 96.

39. ". . . autonomous man—the inner man, the homunculus, the possessing demon, . . ." BFD, p. 191.

40. BFD, pp. 189-90.

41. These for Skinner are the reinforcers and behavior patterns. See BFD, p. 121.

42. This is not to say that all cultural traits are pragmatic or adaptive, any more than that all genetic characteristics have survival value. Some are merely "carried" by adaptive traits. It is interestingly relevant to our later critique of Skinner to see his inability to give a further account of this "carrying" of non-adaptive cultural traits. That the parallel between genetic and cultural inheritance breaks down at this point suggests that Skinner's interpretations may be half-truths.

43. Or "pole."

44. "Just as we do not need to explain the origin of a genetic mutation in order to account for its effect in natural selection, so we do not need to explain the origin of a cultural practice in order to account for its contribution to the survival of a culture." BFD, pp. 129-30. And again, "A given culture evolves as new practices arise, possibly for irrelevant reasons, and are selected by their contribution to the strength of the culture as it 'competes' with the physical environment and with other cultures." BFD, p. 137.

45. See BFD, p. 155.

46. BFD, p. 116.

47. Italics added.

48. PR, p. 155.

49. The modern "philosopher-kings."

50. The limits of which are culturally defined! Notice how the "turn on, drop out" solutions to the problems of the 'sixties could not be assimilated by action-oriented American society, whereas the sit-in, the protest march, and the boycott, once a tool of a radical minority, are now utilized as devices to change anything from anti-abortion laws to the price of meat.

51. See note 36.

52. PR, p. 65.

53. PR, p. 75.

54. See BFD, p. 11.

55. See BFD, pp. 9-12.

56. BFD, p. 13—i.e., inner man, his character, attitudes, emotions, purposes, valuations, etc.

57. "It would be foolish to deny the existence of that private world, but it is also foolish to assert that because it is private it is of a different nature from the world outside. The difference is not in the stuff of which the private world is composed, but in its accessibility." BFD, p. 182.

58. BFD, p. 35.

59. BFD, p. 98.

60. BFD, p. 101.

61. BFD, p. 102.

62. *Ibid.*

63. BFD, pp. 98-99.

64. BFD, pp. 182-83.

65. BFD, p. 186. The unexpressed hope seems to be that if you stop looking at mind, perhaps it will go away.

66. ". . . a person is a member of a species shaped by evolutionary contingencies of survival, displaying behavioral processes which bring him under the control of the environment in which he lives, and largely under the control of a social environment which he and millions of others like him have constructed and maintained during the evolution of a culture. The direction of the controlling relation is reversed: *a person does not act upon the world, the world acts upon him.*" BFD, pp. 201-202. Italics added.

67. BFD, p. 190.

68. See *The Collected Papers of Charles Sanders Peirce*, edd. Charles Hartshorne and Paul Weiss (Cambridge: The Belknap Press of Harvard University Press, 1965), 1.213.

69. BFD, p. 197.

70. "Men have already changed their genetic endowment by breeding selectively and by changing contingencies of survival, and they may now begin to introduce mutations directly related to survival. For a long time, men have introduced new practices which served as cultural mutations, and they have changed the conditions under which practices are selected. They may now begin to do both with a clearer eye to the consequences." BFD, pp. 198-99.

71. See BFD, pp. 204-205.

72. BFD, p. 185.

73. "The creative artist may manipulate a medium until something of interest *turns up.*" BFD, p. 185. Italics added.

74. The language of "conscious monad" in no way implies a new homunculus. It is the last node of intersection of the manifold sub-societies which constitute the structured society of the body. Its Actual World is primarily that portion of the society of neurons in the brain which is receiving the most input from the central nervous system, which itself receives input from the other bodily systems, from the sense receptors, and ultimately from the external environment. The conscious or regnant monad is the center point of a nest of concentric sub-societies (atomic, molecular, cellular, organic, systemic) each of which provides an ordered environment for its included sub-societies.

75. PR, p. 340.

76. "Inner" and "outer" are not to be taken as terms indicating a sharp demarcation between organism and environment. The organism "shades off" into the environment.

77. PR, p. 335.

78. PR, p. 83.

79. In an anthropomorphic analogy, a shivering person relates himself to the heat of a fire, paying no attention to its brightness or color except insofar as they are functions of its heat.

80. PR, pp. 339-40.

81. "One task of a sound metaphysics is to exhibit final and efficient causes in their proper relation to each other." PR, p. 129.

82. Before the concrescence reaches satisfaction, the subject *is not*.

83. "The settled world provides the 'real potentiality' that its many actualities be felt compatibly. . . . The perspective is provided by the elimination of incompatibilities." PR, p. 227.

84. PR, p. 342.

85. PR, pp. 47-48.

86. PR, p. 160.

87. The term "intensity" Whitehead borrows from aesthetics. It is difficult to define but can rather readily be exemplified. A melody, in which the various tones achieve a unity through their incorporation in the overall pattern and sub-patterns of the theme, achieves a higher degree of intensity than a vibrating tuning fork. Intensity is a function of the patterned unity of the satisfaction: of the ways in which discordant elements find their place within it as contrasts or are dismissed in negative prehensions, and of the novelty of the pattern achieved. It is the subjective form of value-achievement.

88. The "in-itself-ness" of a satisfaction.

89. The "for-the-other-ness" of a satisfaction.

90. "The 'subjective' aim, which controls the becoming of a subject, is that subject feeling a proposition with the subjective form of purpose to realize it in that process of self-creation." PR, p. 37.

91. In the interest of accuracy, it must be pointed out that the intensity of the satisfaction is not the subject's feeling of the satisfaction—this would add another element to the satisfaction. Intensity is the internality, the subjectivity of the satisfaction.

92. And "environment" includes past occasions in the personal thread of the subject.

93. PR, p. 375.

94. ". . . emotions, valuations, purposes, adversions, aversions, consciousness, etc." PR, p. 35.

95. Again despite the language of emotion, Whitehead is not referring to conscious processes but to the sort of non-conscious experience which forms the basis of a concrescence.

96. "The philosophies of substance presuppose a subject which then encounters a datum, and then reacts to the datum. The philosophy of organism presupposes a datum which is met with feelings and progressively attains the unity of a subject." PR, p. 234.

97. To take an example from the realm of conscious feelings: a person does not *react to* the efficiency of an insult *with* a feeling of anger. He feels the insult *angrily*.

98. "The many feelings, derivatively felt as alien, are transformed into a unity of aesthetic appreciation immediately felt as private." PR, p. 323.

99. PR, p. 235.

100. The efficient causality of the data.

101. Subjective.

102. PR, p. 323.

103. PR, p. 363.

104. Although novelty is an element in any feeling. "The feeling is always novel in reference to its data; since its subjective form, though it must always have reproductive reference to the data, is not wholly determined by them." PR, p. 355.

105. Phenomena such as energy flow are instances of processes which never get beyond this point.

106. The condition produced in the structured society of the body by an element in the environment.

107. This includes as data both the bodily condition and the environmental agent.

108. PR, p. 75.

109. PR, p. 375.

110. PR, p. 529.

111. PR, p. 531.

112. PR, p. 529.

7

Communitas and *Polis*

Aldo Tassi

In political philosophy today, a number of writers have arisen to challenge the validity of the political order itself. These thinkers, calling themselves anarchists or libertarians, have engaged in analyses of the concept of the state, and they have concluded that the concept has no validity. They maintain that the political order has been exposed as a contradictory state of affairs. Just as a contradictory proposition is one which fails ultimately in its attempt to be a statement about anything, so, they hold, the state fails in its attempt to be a ground whereon human freedom achieves a stable mode of expression. The usual procedure in these discussions is to show that the obligation to obedience which defines the individual's status as citizen is incompatible with the acknowledgment of that same individual's liberty.

What is interesting is that these writers often indicate that it is possible for human freedom to achieve a stable mode of expression in an order other than the political. This new order, which I shall call the communal order, is understood to be related to the political order in a peculiar way: the existence of the political order "hides" and "frustrates" the existence of the communal order. The exposure of the inauthenticity of the former order points to the authenticity of the latter. The state, in other words, is a parasitical reality which has no genuine life of its own. And an individual's status as citizen is not a *sui generis* valid mode of being free. Being a citizen is incompatible with the individual's more fundamental status as a person.

My intention in this essay is to challenge this judgment. I should like to discuss the possibility of distinguishing the notion of a *polis* from the notion of a *communitas*. Such a distinction would be correlative to the distinction between a citizen and a person. I shall attempt to make this distinction by constructing two models—that of the *polis* and that of the *communitas*—wherein I believe it will be clear that the political order constitutes a valid answer to the problem of human freedom.

In virtue of the enormous complexity of the problem of human freedom, it would be foolhardy to attempt a frontal attack on it. What I propose to do is, rather, to discuss human freedom in terms of the notion of mortality. Although, admittedly, this is an unusual approach, I believe nevertheless that it can be justified. That I shall one day not be is the sort of realization which disrupts the rhythm of my life. My life loses its "taken-for-granted" character. To be sure, my life as an organic process with its *natural* rhythm continues; but this serves only to throw into relief the vulnerability of the *human* rhythm of my life which is disrupted. An explanation of death as an organic process is not sufficient to re-establish this rhythm. Natural processes can in no way account for my sense of annihilability. And it is precisely this sense of being annihilable which disrupts the human rhythm of my life. My life becomes pervaded by a sense of meaninglessness. Natural processes belong to the givenness of nature; that is to say, they have their "origin" in that which, so to speak, possesses the character of having "dropped from heaven." Yet the experience of mortality, and the sense of meaninglessness which it brings with it, expose the fact that this character of having "dropped from heaven" is absent from that which constitutes the human dimension of life. The attempt to live a human life transcends, or is not reducible to, that frame of reference wherein clarity consists in understanding oneself and one's behavior as a specimen of a class, or species, in nature. In other words, the humanness of human life is not grounded in nature. Since nature cannot resolve the problem of my mortality, it cannot tell me how I must live. Herein appears the problem of human freedom: how are we to normalize (or stabilize) this status of being beyond the natural rhythm of life? The two models I propose to construct, those of the *communitas* and of the *polis*, will be two ways in which this problem may be resolved.

The first way in which the status of being beyond the natural rhythm of life can be normalized is by positing a *sui generis* reality in each man which is other than his reality as given by nature. This reality is his status as *person*. Each individual finds himself beyond the givenness of nature insofar as he has a sense of being "someone." It is precisely as "someone" that mortality addresses him. In this context, the experience of mortality can be understood to be both a "reminder" and a "warning." As a reminder it turns the individual back toward his "origin" which is not nature. And as a warning it admonishes him that, if he attempts to ground his life in nature, his life will come to nought. He will surrender whatever meaning there may be in the temporal existence which has been given him. In their capacity as persons, individuals come together in a *communitas*, a common "defense." They attempt to create a condition wherein their "origin" as other than nature is able to achieve a "taken-for-granted" character. The essence of a *communitas* is a loving care for him who is threatened. In other words, the purpose of a *communitas* is to provide, in some permanent, stable manner, an "openness" to that someone which each individual is and an "availability" to each individual in virtue of his vulnerability. As such, the *communitas* is a collective witness to the someone each individual is. The *communitas* does not conceive of itself as possessing a life of its own. The only life it acknowledges is the life of the individual person. The validity of the communal order resides in its being the ground in and through which human freedom, understood as constituting the meaning of person, achieves a stable mode of expression.

The second way in which the status of being beyond the natural rhythm of life can be normalized is by positing a *sui generis* reality of which each man is a member. This reality is that of an "historical" species. Men constitute not only a natural species but an historical species. Each individual finds himself beyond the givenness of nature insofar as he has a sense of participating in the life of an historical species. As a member of an historical species, the individual is aware of himself as belonging to a generation. As such, he finds himself "tied" to a past and to a future. In other words, to be a member of an historical species is to partake of a life which is able to encompass past and future generations. The locus, or center, of the life of an historical species is the *polis*. It is in the *polis* that an individual's participation, or membership, in the common life of an historical species achieves a "taken-for-granted" character. This is the individual's status as citizen. In this context, the experience of mortality is resolved in the life of the historical species. The individual dies, but the life in which he partakes as a citizen continues. In the life of an historical species, the individual will be "remembered" after he has died, just as he was "expected" before he was born. The individual overcomes the temporality of his existence in the "eternity" of an historical species. The essence of a *polis* is justice; that is to say, it is the attempt to articulate, in a permanent, stable manner, a common life to which each individual contributes and in the fruits of which each individual shares. Accordingly, the *polis* conceives of itself as possessing a life of its own. And each individual is witness to this common life of an historical species which the *polis* articulates. The validity of the political order resides in its being the ground in and through which human freedom, understood as participation in the life of an historical species, achieves a stable mode of expression.

Before we go on to contrast the notion of a *communitas* with the notion of a *polis*, it is important to notice that a *communitas* is not what we are usually referring to when we speak of a "community." A community, in fact, belongs to the political order. It involves individuals coming together for some positive purpose. They establish a common state of affairs. Each member contributes to the community and, in turn, shares in its benefits. A community, then, possesses the same structure as a *polis*. It is a temporal sub-structure of a *polis*. But it is different from a *polis*. A community has a more or less clear beginning and end. The life of an historical species, however, does not begin or end with it. A community, therefore, is not the locus of an historical species, but rather presupposes a *polis* as the stable background which enables it to achieve its temporal ends.

If we contrast the models of a *communitas* and a *polis*, a very clear and significant difference appears between the communal and political orders. What characterizes the *communitas* is love; what characterizes the *polis* is justice. The relationship which obtains between persons in the *communitas* is one in which the individuals are each acknowledged to be "someone." When I acknowledge another to be a person, his life is present to me in the mode of being *his own* life. This acknowledgment is not made on the basis of some "claim" he has on my life. The obligation I may feel to respond to a need of the other as person is not rooted in an awareness of what is "due" him. Since his needs as a person are radically *his*, there is no objective way of ascertaining, whether correctly or incorrectly, what is "due" him. The obligation which I feel arises, rather, out of my very acknowledgment of him as a person. My "availability" to him in terms of his needs follows from my "openness" to him as a person. Only he can determine what his needs are. The best of intentions notwithstanding, any attempt on my part to determine for him what his needs as a person are constitutes a violation of him as a person. In other words, to acknowledge another as person is to acknowledge the absolute ground for his life as someone. This absolute ground resides in him. The freedom which characterizes a person is not compatible with a determination which has another individual as its source. This also means that the obligation I feel, which follows from my openness to him as a person, has its source in me and not in him. I cannot be coerced to respond to his needs as a person. In the *communitas*, then, each person is an absolute center or locus of freedom. And each relationship between persons is an expression of this freedom. When I acknowledge another as a person, I do so as an expression of my own freedom; and my acknowledgment of the other is directed toward his life as an expression of his own freedom.

The relationship among citizens in the *polis*, however, is one wherein each individual acknowledges a common life in which all of them participate. When I acknowledge another to be a citizen, his life is present to me in the mode of being a "part" of a common life of which I too am a "part." This acknowledgment arises from either a "claim" which he has on my life or a "claim" which I have on his. The basis for such "claims" resides in the fact that we both participate in a common life. This common life is the absolute ground wherein individuals are disclosed as having "rights" and "duties." By virtue of being a member of this common life, each individual stands in a certain relationship to all the other members. This relationship is one of having claims on, and obligations toward, others. Accordingly, a basis exists for ascertaining, whether correctly or incorrectly, what is "due" each of us. In this relationship, unlike that between persons, if I put myself in his place I can understand *what* it is that would be due me. Because we share a common life, it is always possible for me to determine for another what is his due. This, far from being a violation of the other's freedom as a citizen, is the very basis for his claim on me. The source of my obligation toward another is not myself, but the common life in which he and I participate. I enjoy the benefits of this common life; therefore I have an obligation toward others whose contributions I am enjoying. This means that, in the *polis*, unlike the *communitas*, a basis for coercion exists which does not do violence to the freedom of the citizen. As a citizen who is enjoying the benefits of a common life, I find myself having obligations toward others. The coercion which is possible in the *polis* is one which is directed toward a citizen's fulfillment of his obligations. Correlative to the possibility of my understanding what is due another, there is the possibility of the other's understanding what my obligations are. In the *polis*, then, the common life of the historical species is the absolute center or locus of freedom. As a citizen I am beyond the natural rhythm of life in virtue of participating in a life which I share with others. Each relationship between citizens is an expression of this freedom. When I acknowledge another to be a citizen, I do so as an expression of my freedom (my participation in a common life); and my acknowledgment of the other as a citizen is directed toward his life as an expression of his freedom (his participation in the same common life).

An analogy to the distinction between *communitas* and *polis* can be found in the family. On the one hand, the family functions according to the principle of love. There is a total concern for each individual, which is independent of whether the individual is "doing his share" or "receiving his share." On the other hand, the family also functions according to the principle of justice. The attempt is made to ensure that one member of the family does not take undue advantage of the other members. Each is expected to "do his share," and each is entitled to "receive his share." Whether the family functions according to the principle of love or the principle of justice depends upon which truth is being acknowledged in a given relationship: the truth that each individual is a person, or the truth that each individual shares a common life with the others. The dilemmas which arise within the family do so precisely because both principles are valid. Each individual in the family recognizes himself and the others in the family to be persons. And, at the same time, each individual recognizes himself and the others as belonging to a family with its own collective life. This means that the family is at once both a *communitas* and a *polis* in miniature. It is a collective witness to the life each member lives as a person, and each member is a witness to the collective life of the family. The conflict which arises within the family between love and justice does so because each individual in the family *must* live by both principles.

This analogy to the family highlights the ambiguous nature of human freedom. My capacity to transcend the givenness of nature expresses itself both in the fact that I am someone and in the fact that I belong to an historical species in whose life I participate. As such, the communal order and the political order are both articulations of a truth about me. Each order, however, taken individually, leaves unexpressed a fundamental truth about me as a free human being. In order to encompass the total truth about my freedom, both orders are required. Conflicts, nevertheless, may arise between the communal order and the political order. These conflicts do not point to the fact that one order is valid and the other invalid. Rather, what they point to is the ambiguity of human freedom. As such, these conflicts are in the nature of dilemmas. They leave intact the validity of each order.

Both the political and communal orders are grounds wherein a truth about human freedom achieves a stable mode of expression. To argue that the political order is invalid because it is not compatible with the individual's freedom as a person, which is its source, is a misunderstanding. The freedom which is the source of the political order is the freedom which characterizes the citizen, not the person. The political order is simply incapable of addressing itself to individuals as persons. It has nothing to do with human freedom understood as the capacity to be someone. The political order is based on a different truth about human freedom: namely, that every man participates in the life of an historical species. The fact that the political order does not (and cannot) answer the genuine needs of individuals as persons does not impugn in any way the validity of the political order. If it did, then one could argue with equal force that the communal order is invalid because it does not (and cannot) answer the genuine needs of individuals as citizens. Although it is certainly true that justice leaves unresolved the demands of love, it must nevertheless be remembered that it is equally true that love leaves unresolved the demands of justice.

As the distinction between a *communitas* and a *polis* demonstrates, the political order is not a parasitical reality. Its existence does not "hide" or "frustrate" the existence of the communal order. If it is true that today the communal order is "hidden" or "frustrated," this is not the doing of the political order. Rather, the reason lies with the refusal of individuals to stabilize their relationships to each other as persons. Such a stabilization is in no way dependent upon the disappearance of the political order. If the political order were to disappear, the relationships which exist between individuals which are based on justice would become unstable and problematic. This would not point to a more fundamental status of the individual: namely, his status as person. What it would point to instead is the necessity of creating another political order. The demands of justice are simply not the demands of love. Neither can substitute for the other. And both are genuine demands which have their source in human freedom. To be sure, the distinction between a *communitas* and a *polis* does not resolve the dilemma of whether in a given situation the operating principle should be love or justice. The scriptural reference admonishing us to render to Caesar the things that are Caesar's and to God the things that are God's is not so much a solution as a reminder that both love and justice are valid principles by which we *must* live.

8

Interpersonal Dialogue:
Key to Realism

W. Norris Clarke, s.j.

ONE OF THE MOST NAGGING AND PERSISTENT PROBLEMS in the history of epistemology—principally since Descartes and, in a more sophisticated and permanently influential way, since Kant—has been the problem of whether and to what extent we know the external world, the world of the non-self, Kant's noumenon or "thing-in-itself," as it really is in itself. I shall not waste time in recapitulating this all-too-well-known history. Suffice it to say that for Kant—and for a large proportion of modern thinkers in the West since his time—one must indeed posit the *existence* of a real world-in-itself, which acts upon our receptive cognitive faculties of sense to provide the "raw material" on which our minds then impose the *a priori* immanent formal structures of both sense and intellect in order to make these raw data humanly knowable. In a word, the real world provides the matter of our cognition; our own immanent cognitive apparatus, the form.

This is the essence of Kant's "Copernican revolution." Our minds are not, as in Aristotle and the medieval Scholastic realist tradition, a receptive potency, or "matter," as Aristotle calls it, which in knowledge is informed by the forms of real things, projected intentionally into it. The situation is reversed; the world supplies the matter, and we, the form. Our minds are incapable of receiving any prestructured intelligible forms or patterns from outside; all intelligible or meaningful form is from within. The world is incapable, consequently, of revealing itself in any way as it really is to man, and man is incapable of receiving such a revelation and referring it back to its source in a real other, known as such in both its existence and its nature. In a word, there is no objective intentionality from world to man and from man back to world, at least in the dimension of nature, form, or essence—*what* things are in themselves.

It is true that the old, rigid Kantianism, with its apparently timeless and immutable structure of *a priori* forms of sense and understanding the same for all men in all ages, has in our day been transformed into new, more relativistic, linguistic modes. These new linguistic forms still postulate that it is man who imposes his own immanent forms upon the world, but the *a priori* forms now are no longer timeless conceptual ones. They are linguistic structures and systems which are indeed *a priori* for everyone who grows up within them, yet they vary with different cultures and evolve down the ages. The principle that immanent *a priori* forms come from man and not from things is still there, but it has been transposed into the realm of language and, thereby, relativized and historicized. Kant is still very much with us.

I am well aware that there is quite a different and strong current of thought also with us today, that of existential phenomenology, which simply refuses on principle even to raise the "bridge" question of whether or not we know the real world. For such phenomenologists the basic *a priori* of human knowing is an existential situation: we are always already beings-in-the-world, immersed by our world-oriented intentional consciousness in an enveloping real world already given as both other and yet open to our consciousness, a self-revealing world—and all this before we can even raise any theoretical difficulties about the existence or nature of this symbiotic interrelationship, whose givenness is the very condition of the possibility of our raising any questions about it at all. Hence all skeptical, agnostic, or idealist difficulties about our knowledge of the real world always come too late, after the problem has already been solved by our pre-reflective lived experience.

There is undoubtedly a great deal of truth in this analysis of the existential situation into which we are already plunged without our having any say about the matter. Still it seems to me that the reflective philosophical mind cannot rest content simply with this *fait accompli*. It would like to know in addition, if possible, just how it is that we do come to know this real world and how it is possible for this to be the case—i.e., the conditions of possibility of the admitted fact. Furthermore, it seems quite possible to inject a considerable dosage of Kantian apriorism and agnosticism into this existential-phenomenology framework. Man might still be the source of all meaning, imposed on the brute givenness of the world, à la Sartre. Such a compromise blend of part existential phenomenology, part Kantianism is in fact the position of not a few today. It seems to me, then, that no matter what school of philosophy one belongs to, the basic Kantian problem of how and how well we know at least the *nature* of the real world around us is still very much with us, and is indeed of its nature one of those central and perennial philosophical problems which no responsible epistemologist or metaphysician can ignore. It is also one that no latest fashion in conceptual revolutions à la Kuhn can long brush under the rug.

In the present article, I intend to propose a defense of epistemological realism which is simultaneously a refutation of the basic Kantian principle that it is man's mind which imposes forms on the world and not the world on him. This defense will be based on a datum of human experience which no reasonable philosopher is in a position to deny, and yet the implications of which seem to have been strangely overlooked in the history of epistemology, most conspicuously in the Kantian and other immanentist traditions. This is the phenomenon of interpersonal dialogue: that is, successful, intersubjective communication through meaningful, mutually comprehended, linguistic dialogue. The two main points I shall make are (1) that the experience of successful dialogue is an incontrovertible fact and provides the strongest evidence we have of a realistic theory of knowledge: namely, that our minds are able to know to a significant degree the nature or intelligible structure of something real outside of our own minds; and (2) that Kantianism is in principle incapable of explaining the two facts implied in the achievement of such dialogue: namely, (a) that we know there are other real persons, other real entities distinct from ourselves whose *natures* we know as pretty much like our own; (b) that we are able to communicate intelligently with them through language, i.e., receive and send messages substantially intact from one to the other.[1]

Let us start with the data of experience. It is a fact which no reasonable philosopher can deny, under pain of abandoning dialogue with his fellow-philosophers and rendering even his denial empty because it is addressed to no one, that (1) we live in a human community of other real persons like ourselves; (2) we communicate meaningfully with them through language; and (3) we know with sufficient assurance that both the above assertions command our reasonable assent. The very fact that Kant himself wrote and had published his *Critique of Pure Reason* is evidence enough that he too accepted these data, at least implicitly, as suppositions which are taken for granted and existentially lived.

Now, the remarkable thing about a genuine human dialogue is that two human beings, each equally real and distinct from the other—and quite evidently aware of this—actually succeed in communicating meaningfully with each other, despite all the physical media and cognitive processing apparatuses which intervene. Thus, in a genuine dialogue (not just two overlapping monologues, as some conversations unfortunately are) one person asks a question, the answer to which he does not know, waits expectantly for an answer, and then experiences himself receiving an incoming answer from the other, an incoming communication of which he knows he is not the author, and which enlightens or *informs* him about something he did not know before. Even without the question-and-answer format, one undergoes in a dialogue the experience of being informed, of learning something new from the other, if only about the other's thoughts, feelings, desires. And this shared communication comes through in a language which both understand, as learned from a common community transcending both of them. No one creates out of whole cloth and teaches to himself a living language.

Such are the data. The epistemological implications of such an existential situation are extremely rich and—astonishingly—systematically ignored not only by Kant but by almost the whole immanentist tradition. Let me unpack these implications one by one.

1) I know—obviously, but we might as well make it explicit —that I as a participant in this dialogue am real, exist, precisely because I am aware of myself actively putting questions, listening, waiting expectantly, receiving, and being enlightened by, the answer. I know myself as agent and patient (recipient).

2) I know the existence of the other participant in the dialogue as real, because I experience myself as positively and determinately acted on, informed, molded in my consciousness in a way which I cannot originate or control, or even anticipate precisely, but must to a significant degree passively receive from an other-than-myself. This immediate awareness of being acted on, of being actively molded by an independent agent not under my control, constitutes to my mind the primary—and I might add indispensable—evidence for any immediate (non-inferential) knowledge of the existence of a real other.[2]

So much even a Kantian might without too much difficulty be induced to admit, if he is limited simply to the assertion of the *existence* of some real other acting on me. Such in fact is the basic condition of possibility of his own theory of the human mind as the imposer of form on "matter" or data actively presented to it by a real world of things-in-themselves. But I part company with Kantianism when it comes to our ability to know the *nature* of these real agents upon us, *what* they are like in themselves independent of our own imposition of sensible and intelligible forms upon them. It is significant to note here that the usual context of a Kantian analysis of knowledge seems to be that of man-the-thinker trying to understand in scientific categories a mute, non-personal, material world opposite him, which provides him only with raw data to be interpreted but which cannot dialogue with him through a shared language. Man alone in such a "dialogue" does all the talking—if only the inner talking of thinking. The world cannot answer back directly if man interprets it to himself incorrectly. It is an agent, but a mute one. Now, in the case of such a one-sided, or at least unequal, "dialogue" between a human person and the sub-personal material world, there may indeed be a certain initial plausibility in supposing that the human knower imposes his own *a priori* forms and categories on the data supplied by the world (although in fact I do not believe that this explanation will stand up long either under a critical examination of the scientific process itself).

3) But the situation is quite different in the case of a dialogue between two human persons carried on in language. When I listen to someone else speaking to me, answering my question, I am not imposing my own *a priori* formal patterns on the raw material of sound coming from him, structuring it any way I wish (or any way my immanent nature demands). His message comes to me precisely *as a message*, already prestructured by the sender into an intelligible, meaningful pattern incarnated in the material medium of sound—a message which I must receive and understand substantially as it already is in the mind and words of the *other real person* if I am to carry on a successful dialogue at all. The whole point here is that to receive a meaningful message in human language is to receive an already structured, formal, and intelligible pattern from a real source outside of me, and already pre-existing in this other. This means that my cognitive faculties are in principle and in fact capable—given the appropriate conditions—of *receiving* already constituted formal structures from the outside basically as they pre-exist independent of my own cognitive activity, and not merely capable of imposing my own forms on amorphous raw data. A similar conclusion could be drawn from an analysis of the even more basic phenomenon of learning an already constituted language from an already established community into which I come. The essence of any communication situation is that two or more real participants share—communicate and receive—substantially the *same* formal message (despite the always present but more or less minor, non-essential, distortion of "noise" in the system).

4) Another immediate implication of the dialogue situation is that the very fact of carrying on a meaningful dialogue with another implies that in understanding the communication of another through a shared language and conceptual framework I thereby and at the same time understand a great deal about the *nature* or kind of being of the other who is communicating and revealing his mind to me; that he is an intelligent being communicating through linguistic symbols as I do—which is not a bad definition of a man.

My conclusion from all this is that the implications of the interpersonal-dialogue situation open an irreparable breach in the fundamental Kantian principle that our minds cannot receive objective form from real things outside of us but can only impose their own forms on the raw data furnished by the real but not-further-knowable-in-itself outside world. The essence of any meaningful communication situation, on the contrary, is that one does receive, as well as communicate, the same formal shared message from one real pole of the dialogue to the other.

Let me hasten to admit, however, in anticipation of the obvious Kantian riposte, that when I receive a message from someone I do indeed attach a certain dosage of personal interpretation—setting it in the context of my own presuppositions, biases, fears, desires, expectations, etc., both conscious and unconscious, adding on my peculiar emotional coloring of the moment. No one receives in a purely neutral, nakedly objective, way a message of any existential significance from another real person—though one might, of course, in such purely formal matters as logic and mathematics.

All this is true—and one reason why the realism we are defending must be called a "moderate" realism and not an exaggerated or pure picture-copy type. But the fact remains that, despite the more or less considerable aura of interpretative coloring which I add, I still receive and understand *substantially the same message* as was sent out to me by my interlocutor. Otherwise, there is simply no meaningful *communication* at all; hence, no genuine dialogue. Thus if someone reports to me, "There's a fire in your garage," the aura of additional feelings, implications, etc. in which I clothe this message will indeed be my own, and will differ from those imposed on the same message by another hearer. But the core of the message still gets through in its original substantial identity, as unmistakably prestructured by the sender and so received by me, i.e., a *fire*, and not a flood, in *my garage*, and not in your kitchen.

In the light of all this, it seems to me that there is simply no denying the basic aptitude of my cognitive faculties, at least in the privileged—but extremely common—context of interpersonal dialogue, to be receptive of already prestructured formal patterns pre-existing outside of me, formal patterns which are communicated to me in and through my sense faculties, but also understood by my mind. My total reception of any message in a dialogue is thus an inextricable blend of objective and subjective, but with the essential core a shared objective form.

INABILITY OF KANTIANISM TO EXPLAIN DIALOGUE

The more one reflects on the powerful, realistic implications of successful interpersonal dialogue, the more one is astonished to discover that Kant and the entire subjective idealist tradition seem quite oblivious of the whole dimension of interpersonal communication. Nowhere does Kant take up just how it is possible for our minds, structured as he claims, to know that other human persons, like us in their inner make-up (i.e., in their intrinsic natures or essences), exist at all in the real world. Nor does he undertake to explain how two such beings are capable of carrying on meaningful communication with each other through a common shared language, learned by both as already prestructured by a previously existing community. There seems to be no way I can see in which his system could absorb such data of our everyday experience. Yet it is perfectly obvious that he is constantly presupposing both these facts, taking them for granted, by the very fact of taking active part, as he did, in philosophical dialogue with his contemporaries and writing his books in the German language precisely in order to get his carefully prestructured message across accurately to them and to convince them of its truth for and about all his fellow-men.

He does indeed assert as part of his system that all human minds have a similar structure of sensible and intellectual forms and categories, and that that is how we can agree on the common structuring of the material world which we call true or objective human knowledge. But this still does not account for the fact *that* or *how* we know that in fact such other similarly structured human knowers exist at all for us to dialogue with, and just how we are able, on his principles, to communicate successfully with them by trans-subjective messages in a trans-subjective common language. There simply is no theory in Kant of interpersonal knowledge or communication—nor, it seems to me, can there be in principle—yet the acceptance of the fact is the very presupposition of the attempt to write down and communicate the doctrine which would render such knowledge and communication impossible. Quite a paradoxical situation! But

surely it is not the first time such a situation has turned up in the
history of philosophy.

It would be a fascinating and, I am sure, illuminating explora-
tion in the history of ideas to examine how other philosophers in
the general Kantian and allied subjective idealist traditions have
handled the problem of the knowledge of other persons and of
interpersonal dialogue. But I have not the space to do this here.
It is enough to recall the extreme difficulties of the idealist-phase
of Husserl in our own century in trying to account, by an immanentist theory of the constitution of the object by the transcendental ego, for the knowledge of other personal egos as real and
for their meaningful linguistic communication with each other.
It is surely not by chance that we observe one after the other of
these thinkers either quietly bypassing the whole question or else
landing in extreme difficulties in trying to remain consistent with
their own Kantian or subjectivist principles. And for good reason, it seems to me. No theory of the purely immanent constitution of either the existence or the nature of all the objects of our
cognition can possibly, so far as I can see, cope with the un-
yielding evidence of the everyday fact of interpersonal dialogue:
that we do, in fact, in every meaningful dialogue receive into our
consciousness from outside our minds an already prestructured
formal pattern constituted substantially by another, notwithstanding the accompanying coloring of subjective interpretation
which we superimpose without destroying the clearly recogniz-
able substance of the message. In a word, successful interpersonal
dialogue demands a basic, though carefully qualified, realism in
epistemological explanation. And Kantianism is incapable of providing it.

OUR KNOWLEDGE OF THE NON-PERSONAL WORLD

I should like now to push the epistemological implications of
dialogue a decisive step farther, to include with new qualifica-
tions our realistic knowledge not only of the existence—which
Kant himself would admit—but also of the nature of the *non-
personal* material world surrounding us. Once we have broken
through the basic Kantian principle and established that our cognitive faculties can in fact be thus receptive of already constituted form from the outside—at least in this one extremely com-

mon type of situation, namely, interpersonal dialogue—then what is there in principle to prevent them from being receptive also of other formal structures already pre-existing in real non-personal things outside our minds and communicated to us by their non-linguistic, but just as determinately structured, action on our senses? If we are able in one case to receive a previously structured formal pattern substantially as it is in its source outside of us, why should we not be able to do something similar in other cases as well, as long as there is a pre-existent formal structure somehow already there either by art or by nature—does it matter much which?—and it is communicated to us by an appropriately structured action? For no real action is simply amorphous, indeterminate, totally determinable by its recipient. This is really a contradiction in terms. It follows that all action, as structured and determinate, must to some significant degree be a communication system, conveying something of the active agent to the at least partially passive recipient. Once Kant has admitted that our cognitive faculties are in any way receptive of, actuated or determined by, the action of another, so that we can and must affirm its real existence, he cannot consistently deny that these same faculties are at the same time receptive of the formal patterns which inevitably structure all determinate action.

The alert reader, however, will scarcely need the prodding of a Kantian objector to notice the significant difference between the linguistic communications of an interpersonal dialogue and the non-linguistic communications of the non-personal material world to us. He might well object thus: granted that we are able to receive from the outside formal structures of meaning encoded in language, the reason why we can share these same meanings is that we know how to reproduce similar meanings within ourselves by our own conceptual–linguistic activity. But we cannot do this with the formal structures communicated to us by the action of non-personal agents, for neither the content nor the mode of communication is linguistically expressed meanings. We have no way of knowing how the coded patterns into which we transpose all their actions on us correspond to the original formal structures in the thing itself, or what such structures are actually like in their source, since we cannot reproduce them in our consciousness as we can linguistic patterns. We have to translate into our own human coding systems whatever we receive from the outside.

This is quite true. All the structured action-patterns we receive from the outside have to be transposed into our own information-coding systems, which do not in any way directly resemble as an immediate picture-copy the formal patterns as imbedded in their original sources—and even if they did, there is no way we could know this. But the fact remains that no matter how much a message is coded, recoded, transposed into different coding media, the whole point of any successful information-coding operation is that there is a determinate formal pattern in the coded message as received which matches and is positively determined by an isomorphic formal pattern in the sender, though, of course, the respective material embodiments of these isomorphic formal structures in sender and receiver do not have to match. A code after all *is* a code, i.e., an informative communication system.

All that is needed, it seems to me, for a successful "moderate" realist explanation of human knowledge is that there be a fixed determinate correlation between the formal structure of the coded communications we receive in our senses and intellects from the material world, on the one hand, and some substantially isomorphic formal structure in the same real world, on the other, even though we can never contact the latter nakedly in itself without the intermediary of our own coding system. This isomorphic correlation of formal structures, determined by the action of the sender on the receiver, and not vice versa, is all we need to construct bit by bit a detailed human-scale map of the world in which we are immersed in a constant "dialogue" of interaction. Such a map is certainly not as detailed as the real world is in itself, and not on the same scale. But it is informative and accurate enough for our needs and purposes. What we have, therefore, in our experimentally tested knowledge of the non-personal material world around us, is a substantially isomorphic map of this world, re-created in our consciousness on a human scale in terms of our own peculiar coding system, but according to a steady flow of coded communications whose formal properties are not imposed by us, à la Kant, but received from and determined by the world itself.

This, to my mind, is the essence of "moderate" realism—a

realism which is at its strongest when we are dealing with the knowledge of other human persons like ourselves and with interpersonal linguistic dialogue, and which tapers off with increasing qualification as we descend farther from man into the sub-personal world, but without ever breaking the umbilical cord which links our knowledge to this world by the communication system of action.

To sum up: the basic phenomenon of human dialogue, involving as it does the trans-subjective sharing of a common background of meanings and symbols learned from others, plus the sharing of a substantially identical formal message between two real poles, sender and receiver, is the strongest evidence we have for a realistic theory of knowledge, and thereby opens an irreparable breach in the fundamental Kantian principle that the real world supplies only the matter and our minds the form of our human knowledge. Once we have broken through this Kantian principle that our cognitive faculties cannot receive formal structures already pre-established independently of us, the path is open for a "moderate" realist theory of knowledge even of the non-personal material world, through the medium of the universal communication system of action, within the matrix of the interaction of the world and ourselves.

NOTES

1. My first insight into the role of language and dialogue in providing especially powerful evidence for realism came from the exploitation of this theme by August Brunner, s.j., one of the pioneers among Catholic thinkers in the personalist movement in Germany, and also one of my professors during my first philosophical studies in France. See his *La connaissance humaine* (Paris: Aubier, 1943), *La personne incarnée* (Paris: Beauchesne, 1947), and *Die Grundfragen der Philosophie: ein systematischer Aufbau* (Freiburg: Herder, 1933), later published as *Fundamental Questions of Philosophy*, trans. Sidney A. Raemers (St. Louis: Herder, 1937). My views on the subject developed through contact with other personalist thinkers, such as Gabriel Marcel, Martin Buber, Emmanuel Mounier, etc. When my own reflections are added, I can now no longer distinguish these later influences from my own unfolding of the initial clue, for which I gladly pay tribute to Father Brunner.

2. Let me indicate here, without development, the basic general thesis of my whole epistemology: *all* knowledge of the real is an interpretation of action, either of myself as acting or of myself as being acted on, plus the implications thereof.

9

Person, Community, and
Moral Commitment

Robert O. Johann

My aim in this paper is to explore the nature and grounds of moral commitment. Is morality ultimately a matter of arbitrary partisanship, as some contemporary ethicists are saying? [1] Or does it have a basis in the nature of things? [2] Is there an objective moral order binding on all men regardless of the way they think or feel about it, or are moral norms simply cultural constructs which derive whatever validity they enjoy solely from the allegiance given them in particular times and places? [3]

The question is a large one, but the times in which we live make it urgent. For these times manage to combine an extraordinary degree of moral activism on the level of practice with an all-but-dogmatic brand of ethical nihilism on the level of theory. On the one hand, all our inherited ways, traditions, and institutions are being subjected to unrelenting criticism with a view to their radical transformation. Absolutely nothing is sacred. On the other, there is the widespread denial of any basis in reality for judging one way of life to be morally superior to another, or even for preferring the moral standpoint to some other in evaluating proposed courses of action. [4] The situation is nothing short of absurd. If ethical nihilism is true, then obviously any kind of genuine renewal or reform is out of the question. The only thing possible is a succession of different behavioral patterns with that one carrying the day which happens to have the strongest proponents. Anything like a rational consensus, the achievement of social cooperation on the basis of insight rather than by force or psychological conditioning—tactics which, not surprisingly, are being increasingly advocated[5]—becomes an idle dream. Man is condemned to endless strife without even the possibility, much less the hope, of real reconciliation.

With the supposed inevitability of such a state of affairs this paper takes issue. Nihilism is the fruit not of insight into the human condition but of blindness to its essential structure. This blindness stems in part from the common identification of objective reality with the findings of scientific inquiry. As Dewey noted long ago, such an identification cannot but result in the denial of objective import to value judgments in general and to moral judgments in particular, and in their relegation to the realm of the private and subjective.[6] But, as the said identification is arbitrary, so the conclusion is unwarranted. Indeed, as will be shown, if science were our only access to the real, there could not even be such a thing as science.[7] What is needed, therefore, is a fresh look at the problem, a look undistorted by the prejudice that "scientific" and "objective" are synonyms. In the following pages, I propose to take such a look.

The first part of the paper will be devoted to an analysis of the logical structure of value judgments in general. Here I shall stress their intrinsic dependence on human interest while indicating at the same time why such dependence is not an obstacle to their genuine, even if sometimes limited, objectivity. In the second part, I shall seek to uncover the transcendental interest which defines the human as such and is the objective basis for universally valid judgments of moral value. As we shall see, man is not just a collection of atomic individuals, but an ever-to-be-created community of persons, and the interest in achieving such community is the wellspring and ground of authentic human existence. The moral order thus has its roots in the essentially interpersonal structure of man's life, and it is this structure which grounds the possibility of objectively valid appraisals of human conduct.

I. JUDGMENTS OF VALUE

Following the lead of Bernard Lonergan,[8] I shall start by saying that a judgment of value is an answer to a question for deliberation.

It is an answer to a *question*, first of all. This is true of any judgment. Judgment comes at the end of inquiry and presupposes the inquiry it terminates. Secondly, it is the answer to a question for *deliberation*. This is to distinguish it from a purely intellectual judgment which answers a question for reflection. The inquiry preceding intellectual judgments intends reality simply as it is. It is concerned with the way things are, regardless of the aims and intentions of the inquirer. Deliberation, on the other hand, looks precisely to the realization of those aims and interests. As an answer to a question for deliberation, the value judgment is a determination of an action or choice in line with those aims. Whereas reflective inquiry organizes what presents itself to consciousness into an object for intellect, deliberative inquiry, on the basis of what is known (about both the facts of the situation *and* the intentions of the inquirer), determines a *project* for will. Its term is not an object, but a principle of action or choice which is grasped as consistent with an end already aimed at. The intention of an end is thus presupposed in any deliberative process. Unless we should find ourselves already intent on some objective and at the same time doubtful about the ways and means of reaching it, deliberation would never arise and value judgments never be made. For value judgments are always, at least implicitly, about the steps to be taken to realize a goal to which the judger is already committed.

I call attention to this intrinsic connection between what is judged and the interests of the judger because it is the distinctive feature of value judgments. The end already intended is both the wellspring of the deliberative process and the standard for carrying it out. Its attractiveness to the inquirer is what motivates his efforts, whereas its being the sort of end it is enlightens and guides them. Because the end is what it is (and the situation in which it is to be realized is the way it is), only certain steps are rationally called for (i.e., are good to take). Just what they are (i.e., the determination of what is good in the situation) is a function of the relationship between intending them and intending the end. Only insofar as that relationship is one of consistency can the projected steps be affirmed as what it is good (or rational) to do. The end already intended by the inquirer thus serves as the basis or standard for the value judgments which conclude his inquiry. No value judgment is possible without the prior adoption of such a standard.

To say this, however, is not to say that adopted standards may never be questioned or that, since deliberation is always about ways and means to an end, we never deliberate about ends themselves. As a matter of fact, any unconditional approval of a "means" always involves a reapproval of the end toward which it is directed. To judge an act as worthwhile *because* of the interest it promotes is at the same time to reaffirm the interest itself as one worth pursuing. But the point I am making is that when we are deliberating about ends and trying to decide what goals we should commit ourselves to and in what order of priority, we are weighing these possible ends and goals themselves as the means to something we are already bent on achieving. They are, if you like, formal (or directive) means, as distinct from material (or effective) means. And their evaluation, like any evaluation, presupposes an already intended end in the light of which they are being appraised. In other words, the deliberate choice of "ends," no less than the deliberate choice of "means," is possible only in relation to a goal to which the chooser has already committed himself.

For this reason, value judgments are in a sense more significant for what they imply than for what they expressly assert. For a value judgment, although expressly about what is to be done, is more fundamentally about the judger himself. To say unconditionally that something is good or bad is implicitly to affirm that I, who make the claim, am bent on a goal in the light of which the appraisal is made. It is to acknowledge that I am the sort of person who not only finds such a goal attractive but who has committed himself to its realization. If, as Aristotle claims, the kind of person we are determines the kind of things we will find good, the converse is also true. The judgments we make about good and bad determine the kind of person we are. They are implicit ratifications of the interests which shape our lives. And this meaning, even though implicit, is more fundamental than what is expressly asserted, because it is, as I have tried to show, the latter's ground.

If this is the case, however, then how can judgments of value lay any claim to objectivity? If the ground of such judgments is located in the commitment of the judger, then are they not, as is so often claimed, simply disguised statements of personal bias and without objective warrant? For, the objectively real is that, the nature of which is not dependent upon what anyone thinks about it, but which presents itself instead as the measure of thought and the basis of rational consensus. Since to attain objectivity is to grasp *what is* regardless of whether we like what we find or not, the pursuit of objectivity would seem to require setting our likes and dislikes aside. And yet, as the analysis so far would indicate, a value judgment, far from prescinding from such likes and dislikes, actually presupposes them as its basis.

The idea that to be objective a judgment must prescind from the interests of the judger is, although widespread, simply mistaken. If one wants to know reality as it is, apart from any interest one might take in it, obviously one must keep such interests from intruding into one's inquiry. Such, for example, is the aim and procedure of the empirical sciences. But if one wants to know what it is good to do or choose, then just as obviously those interests are intrinsic to the inquiry. In either case, the result of the inquiry, if it is successful, will be a judgment about *what is*, and one which calls for the assent of anyone inquiring into the matter at hand.

In order to make this point clear, it will be helpful if I distinguish between two aspects of any interest or commitment or, more generally, of any intentional act. In any intention, there are two poles: there is the subject actively intending (the subjective pole) and there is that which is intended (the objective pole). In the language of the Scholastics, the distinction is between the *intentio intendens* and the *intentio intenta*. And if the word "interest" is substituted for intention, what we have is a distinction between subjective interest, or interest viewed from the side of the subject who is actively interested in something, and objective interest, which is what some subject is actually interested in. The two terms of this polarity are clearly inseparable and mutually dependent. There is no *intentio intenta* without an *intentio intendens*, and vice versa; there are no objective interests without subjective interests, and vice versa. And, applying this to what I was saying above, there is no end (i.e., an *intentio intenta*) unless there is someone actually committed to it, actually intending it (i.e., an *intentio intendens*). In this sense, the intending of an end is the ground of that end's being an end. Yet no one can actually intend something unless that something is such as to be able to terminate an actual intention of it. Nothing cannot be practically intended.

Now when I said above that the logical ground of a value judgment is the commitment of the judger, I meant his commitment in the objective sense, commitment as *intentio intenta*, objective interest, intended end. As I just explained, it cannot be an intended end for him unless he actually intends it. Or to put it another way (and recalling that the intended end of the inquirer is the standard for the judgment which concludes his inquiry), a standard cannot serve as a standard for someone unless he himself adopts it as a standard. But it is not *my* adoption of a standard or *my* intending an end which grounds the judgment made with respect to it; it is the adopted standard itself, the intended end itself, which does this. For it is precisely with respect to the adopted standard, the intended end, that the judgment is made. The judgment that something is good, therefore, will be valid if the projected action (implicit in such a judgment) is actually consistent with the objective interest of the judger. And this validity is something objective, since anyone who shares that interest—i.e., intends the same end— -will, if he inquires into the thing in question, be required to make the same judgment in its regard. In other words, a value judgment, although implicitly about the judger (as I have explained), is not directly about him but about what is judged. It is a judgment on the relation between one objective content (the projected end) and another objective content (the objective interest of the judger). And the judgment is objectively valid if the relation affirmed actually holds.

From this it should be clear that judgments of value are not simply expressions of taste or personal preference, even though such expressions are often put in the form of value judgments.[9] For example, I may say that something is good when what I really mean is that I like it, that I find it appealing. Insofar as such a statement is a judgment at all, it is the answer to a question for reflection, not for deliberation—a question in the form: What, as a matter of fact, is my attitude toward this object? Do I find it good (i.e., appealing, satisfying, an object of liking) or not? If I say I like it, or find it good in this sense, clearly I am not evaluating the object but simply describing my reaction to it. To evaluate something is to answer a question about its worth, a question for deliberation. It is to answer, for example, the question: Is this object, which may be good in the sense that I like it, really good, i.e., something which it is rational to want? And as we have seen, such a question arises only for one who is already bent on a specific goal to the accomplishment of which the object in question is in some way relevant—it being the purpose of the deliberative process to determine in just what way.

A specific (although not always expressly specified) goal, functioning as the standard for evaluating the object, is thus always involved in a judgment of value about it (which is not the case with mere expressions of taste). That is why, although I may like something and you may not, a true judgment about its worth, *if made with respect to the same standard*, must be the same for us both. It cannot be that the same project is both consistent and inconsistent with one and the same end. When our appraisals of the same thing differ, they both cannot be valid unless we are applying different standards of evaluation. In that case, although we are considering the same object, we are not asking the same question about it. We are questioning the relation of its projected use or whatever in relation to different goals; and, it is clear, in relation to different goals, one and the same project can be both good and bad—and objectively so.

This is all very well, a reader may say, but it does not get us very far. Consider a concrete example. A group of white people, angered at a decision by school authorities to bus more black children from the ghetto into their already "integrated" school, propose to close it down by a sit-in. From their point of view, the proposal which calls public attention to their grievance looks like a good thing. For the authorities, anxious to keep the school open and running smoothly, it is a bad thing. For the black parents, who want their children to have the advantages of a better school, it is a bad thing. For some of the schoolchildren, who like nothing better than a holiday, it is a good thing. Now, according to the theory so far presented, all these evaluations are objectively valid, insofar as the relation of consistency/inconsistency between the sit-in and the objective interests of the various groups actually holds. The sit-in is a way for two groups to get what they want, and it prevents two other groups from getting what they want. Yet what does anyone who insists that value judgments are ultimately subjective mean to say other than that, when it comes to making such judgments, such a situation as the one just described can prevail? Here you have different groups evaluating the sit-in in contrary ways, and doing so, not because of anything in the nature of a sit-in, but because of the conflicting interests they bring to the situation. Are not value judgments called subjective precisely because there are no objective means for settling disputes about them? Yet why be concerned about objectivity at all if not for the possibility it affords of our reaching a rational consensus, i.e., a coordination of our activities on the basis of insight into the real rather than by force or psychological arm-twisting?

This objection is admittedly fatal to any claim for the complete adequacy of what has been said so far. Indeed, my recognition of the need to say more is the reason why the present paper has two parts instead of just one. However, the points I have tried to make are crucial to what follows and should, therefore, be kept in mind. (1) Any deliberative inquiry presupposes an already intended end which functions as the standard for its successful resolution. (2) The presence of personal interest as a determining factor in such inquiry does not, contrary to a widespread assumption, preclude the objective validity of the conclusions it reaches. If, as in our example, that validity happens to be limited, it is not because interests are dominant, but because the dominant interests are particular and contingent. This means that philosophers in search of a basis for universal consensus in the realm of values are making a mistake when they look for it in the findings of science, which prescinds from interests.[10] It will not be by moving away from interests in the direction of bare facts that the solution will be found, but only by moving through empirical and contingent interests to an interest which lies beyond them, if indeed there be such. To this question we must now direct our attention.

II. MORAL COMMITMENT

The problem which faces us is that of resolving conflicts of interest on a rational basis. When individuals and groups bring divergent objective interests to the same situation, is there any possibility of rationally adjudicating them, or can value disputes be settled only by bashing heads? To put it another way: if objective interests ground the choice of means to their fulfillment, is there anything to ground the choice of those interests themselves, i.e., the choice of what ends to pursue and what standards to adopt? If not, then clearly we are left with the kind of situation described in our example. Our commitments are a matter of happenstance, and the value judgments we make in their light, though valid in relation to them, are infected with their arbitrariness. In the realm of value, there will be genuine communication only between those who *happen* to share the same goals.

A first step toward answering the questions just raised has already been made. We have seen that all deliberation is about the ways and means to an already intended end. If we deliberate about interests or ends, we are weighing their adoption or pursuit as directive means for realizing a goal we are already aiming at. Conflicting interests, therefore, can be rationally adjudicated only on the basis of another interest, to the fulfillment of which their pursuit or rejection is relevant. This other interest, however, if it is to support the burden we are placing on it, cannot be of the same order as the interests being judged in its light. That is to say, it itself cannot be an interest which can come into rational conflict with other interests and so itself stand in need of adjudication. Since any limited or restricted interest is open to such conflict, the interest which provides the basis for resolving all conflicts of interest must transcend all limits and restrictions. It must in this sense be a transcendent interest.

In the pages which follow, then, I shall first sketch out some of the formal characteristics of such a transcendent interest. Secondly, I shall raise the question of its existence. Can the existence of such an interest be rationally affirmed? Finally, I shall try to formulate its content. For a transcendent interest can fulfill its role in settling disputes only if it is publicly available and generally accepted, and it can be such only if it has first been formally objectified.

First of all, then, the unrestricted or transcendent interest which could serve as the standard for resolving all questions of value would itself have to be *unquestionable*. Not only would it be an interest which is not questioned as a matter of fact. (Many of our actual interests are of this sort. We reaffirm them implicitly in the judgments we make in their light; they become routine, and we do not raise questions about them.) But our transcendent interest would be had or experienced as itself not open to questioning. Otherwise it could not be grasped as the truly final standard.

Secondly, the interest or intended end I am talking about would have to be a *necessary* end, i.e., necessarily intended, both from the side of the intending subject (subjectively) and from the side of the object (objectively). If the interest were not subjectively necessary, it would be for the subject a contingent affair and open to choice. But what is open to choice is subject matter for deliberation, and what is subject matter for deliberation is not unquestionable. Yet what is had as unquestionable is also had as rationally compelling or objectively necessary. It is an interest which cannot be rationally rejected.

Thirdly, as antecedent to choice and entering into the very constitution of the subject as such, this interest will be one in which all subjects share, an end which all intend; it will be *universal*. And as rationally compelling for all rational subjects, it must be something whole, all-inclusive, incapable of being subordinated to anything beyond itself, *absolute*. It will indeed be the fulfillment of each subject as such and the fulfillment of all subjects together.

Now, if there is such an interest as this, it means that there is such a thing as *normative* human nature. It means that man by nature *is* the intention of an end in relation to which all his choices can be weighed. Moreover, since this is what is required if disputes about value are to be settled rationally, it is perfectly clear that any attempt to bypass the idea of man's nature in dealing with this issue is doomed to failure. The fact that most contemporary ethicists give short shrift to it is, I contend, the reason why on this point they make no headway at all.[11] They think that there is no evidence for the existence of a nature which could function in this way. That they are mistaken I must now try to show.

The first point to be made is that evidence for human nature as normative will be found only if one looks in the right place for it. For example, it will not be found simply by analyzing the concept of man, as some contemporary ethicists are wont to do.[12] For the concept of man is, as they rightly note, normally employed in a purely classificatory way. "Its field of reference," as Macmurray remarks, "is . . . the class of existents which are identifiable by observation, as possessing the factual characteristics by which objects are assigned to this class." [13] Unlike the concept of something which is defined in terms of its function (e.g., the concept of a knife), the concept of man does not entail any idea of goodness or badness. Since a knife is something fashioned for a specific purpose, to know what a knife is is also to know what qualities it is rational to want in a knife (i.e., what a good knife is). A good knife will be such a knife that a choice of it is consistent with the purpose for which knives are made. In other words, when things are classified in terms of their suitability for achieving a certain goal, the class concept itself provides a norm for distinguishing good and bad specimens of the class. But when things are classified simply on the basis of observable characteristics, regardless of the ends to which they may be put, the class concept is normative only for *identifying* members of the class, not for *evaluating* them. The concept of man is of the latter sort. It does not provide any basis for distinguishing good men from bad. And, so the argument goes, since our concept of man is our grasp of his nature (i.e., of that by which an individual man is what he is and belongs to the class of objects he does), human nature itself contains no clue to human goodness or badness.

Now I will not argue that, although we normally use the concept "man" or "human" in this purely descriptive way, we do not always do so. We sometimes have occasion to say to someone, for example, "Be a man" or "Act like a human being." Such expressions would be pointless, however, if what they meant were "Have the characteristics which, as a man, you are observed to have" or "Behave in ways in which men are observed to behave." It is meaningless to prescribe what is already the case. That is why we do not say to a dog "Be a dog" or "Behave like a dog." For a dog cannot fall short simply as a dog; but (at least such injunctions would seem to imply) a man can fall short—and simply as a man. And if that is the case, then human nature is not adequately grasped if it is identified merely with a set of observable characteristics. Being human is not simply a matter of fact but a task to be accomplished, something which can be done well or poorly. And a good man is one with the dispositions to do it well. "Be a man" then means "Have the dispositions necessary for the accomplishment of the task set by your nature as a man." And "Act like a human being" means "Act in the way in which a man with such dispositions would act."

I say that I will not argue this way (although it seems to me not without merit) because someone will surely retort that the use of such expressions simply means that the one using them has adopted (perhaps from the culture in which he was reared) some ideals of human goodness which serve as his standards of judgment about human behavior. "Be a man" simply means "Have the dispositions prized by the culture in which you live." That the standard is not implied by the very nature of man is sufficiently clear from the fact that the concept "man" can be used merely to classify. In other words, the kind of person I have in mind is convinced from the start that our knowledge of man or of anything else, for that matter, is scientific knowledge, i.e., the kind of knowledge which depends on observation and experiment. If such were the case, then, of course, what we *know* about man would provide no basis for evaluating an individual simply as a man. But such is not the case, and that is what I want to show.

The reason why scientific knowledge is not exhaustive of what we know is that, if it were, there could be no such thing as science. For science occurs only as a result of scientific investigation. Such investigation, however, is not an object in the world; it is an intentional activity, something which men intentionally do. But we cannot do anything intentionally unless we are aware (and, in that sense, know) that we are doing it. The scientist knows himself as scientific investigator in the very act of investigating and not as something found out by investigation. And since such knowledge is a prerequisite for knowledge of the scientific kind, it itself cannot be an instance of it. The same thing can be said about observation. If observation were our only source of knowledge, there could be no such thing as observation, much less knowledge. For to observe is not simply to be staring blankly; it is to be engaged intentionally in the activity of collecting data relevant to some hypothesis. But, again, to be engaged intentionally in an activity is to know oneself as so engaged. The observer knows himself as observer, not by observing himself, but in the very act of making observations.

I stress this kind of knowing as that which science presupposes because it is only on the basis of such knowledge that man's normative nature can be grasped. If man's nature is an intentional reality, an *intentio intendens* (which, as noted above, it must be if our problem is to be solved), it can be known as such, not as something attended to from the outside, but only in its very activity of intending—in *actu exercito*, as the Scholastics would say. Were inquiry needed for this sort of knowledge, not only would it never be possessed, but we could never intentionally do anything. Again, to be looking for this sort of knowledge at the end of an inquiry is to be looking in the wrong place and to be forgetting what one already knows. The evidence for man's normative nature is his consciousness of himself as an intentional subject. And the rational affirmation of such a nature calls for attention to, and understanding of, this consciousness, the objectification of the awareness we have of ourselves when acting, not the analysis of concepts or the observation of the way men behave.

If, therefore, we attend to the consciousness we have of ourselves as intentional subjects, what do we find? Since our problem is with judgments of value, and since such judgments are answers to questions for deliberation, the consciousness we must explore is the consciousness we have when deliberating. What are we consciously about when we engage in deliberation?

To be deliberating is to be trying to make the right choice in a set of possibilities. It is to be aware, therefore, that our choices must meet certain requirements if they are not to be self-frustrating and that these requirements are objective. Our choices will not be right simply because it is we who make them; their rightness depends on their consistency with the end at which we are aiming. To know their rightness is to grasp this consistency, the fact that making them is identical with accomplishing the end insofar as this is possible in the situation. The end being accomplished by our choices is thus their rational basis, their ground.

Now our choices, if they are to be wholly right, need to be grounded in two respects. These two respects correspond to the two poles involved, as we have seen, in any intentional act, the subjective pole and the objective pole. Like any intentional act, a choice may be regarded both from the side of its term, i.e., from the side of what is chosen (which is to regard it objectively), and also from the side of its source, i.e., as a determinate actualization of will (which is to regard it subjectively). Objectively, the choice is a specific project. Subjectively, it is a commitment of a chooser to that project, and so to the end which the project realizes. These aspects, though distinct, are inseparable, and both must be attended to if his choice is to be one which the chooser can wholly approve. However, the bases or grounds for such approval are different in each case. For the choice, objectively considered, is right to the extent that it is consistent with the end for which it is made. But the choice is right subjectively (i.e., as a specific commitment of will), only if it is consistent with, and the realization of, an end to which will is ordered prior to any of its commitments. For, what the chooser must weigh here is the rightness or wrongness of his intending the end he does. And since this intending is his very being and actuality as a subject, it is his very selfhood, the sort of person the choice will make him, which is coming under judgment.

This distinction between those exigencies which impose themselves conditionally (i.e., *if* the chooser happens to be intending a certain end) and those which impose themselves absolutely (because, as the basis for distinguishing the rightness or wrongness of his intentions, they claim his allegiance simply as a subject and prior to any choices he makes) is itself the ground for distinguishing between *technological* rightness or wrongness and *moral* rightness or wrongness. For the reasons given, both dimensions are involved in every choice. Every choice either meets or fails to meet both the exigencies of an empirical end (the end ratified in the act of choosing and regulating the choice objectively considered—i.e., as a choice of means) and the exigencies of a transcendent end (the end intended prior to the act of choosing and regulating the choice subjectively considered—i.e., as a determinate commitment of the chooser). On the first level, we have technological rightness or wrongness; on the second, moral rightness or wrongness. A choice may be wrong in both respects or in either one of them, but only if it is right in both respects is it wholly right. And only if it is at least morally right is the one making it approvable in his reality as a subject. To put it another way: a man may be good but stupid, or intelligent but wicked. The former will fail in his efforts to do the good he wills, but the latter fails in his very being as a man.

I say that we are implicitly aware of all this in any deliberative effort. This means that the distinction between right and

wrong is not something arrived at theoretically. Just as the effort
to understand presupposes the distinction between intelligible and
unintelligible, and the effort to judge presupposes the distinction
between true and false, so the effort to deliberate presupposes
the distinction between right and wrong, and we cannot engage
in deliberation without being directly conscious of it. Moreover,
we could not raise moral, as distinct from technological, questions if we were not already aware of the different ways in
which a choice must be grounded if it is to be wholly right. For,
to raise a question is already to be conscious of that in terms of
which the question is meaningful.[14] Were there no such thing,
not only could the question not be answered; it could not even
be asked. Since to ask a moral question implies the asker's
awareness of, and interest in, an end which transcends his very
being as subject and imposes itself unconditionally upon him, we
can affirm, on the basis of our asking such questions, both the
existence of this end and the existence of our interest in it. To
deliberate morally is to be a conscious interest in a transcendent
end.

Let us look at this a little more closely. Since a transcendent
end is an end for the subject, not by choice, but by nature, it is
something he necessarily shares with all subjects. Moreover, as
that in terms of which his very commitments and life as a subject
are meaningful, it is the ground of all rational action whatsoever
and so cannot be rationally rejected. It is an interest which by its
very nature is unquestionable, incapable of being subordinated to
anything else, absolutely final. In other words, our very capacity
to engage in moral deliberation implies an awareness on our part,
however implicit it remains or however confused by subsequent
theorizing, that our very nature as subjects is normative for our
conduct. Each of us as a subject *is* the intention of a transcendent end which is the rational ground of his being. The nature,
then, which all subjects share is that transcendent interest for
which we have been looking and which alone can serve as the
rational basis for settling the conflicts of interest between subjects.

It remains for us now formally to objectify this interest.
Merely showing that man's nature is the final moral norm is not
enough. We must also come into reflective awareness of what
that nature is if it is to serve as the last court of appeal for settling

the disputes which divide us. How to express to ourselves the content of that interest which is our nature? How to formulate that end to which we are naturally ordered and whose requirements must be met if our choices and we who make them are to be rationally grounded? This is the task I must now take up if the problem with which I started is to have a solution.

The formula we are looking for is implicit in what has gone before. I said earlier that only an end which transcends our acts of choosing and is already an end for us prior to them can ground them. It must be an end by nature and not simply by choice. What I must now bring out is that such an end can be conceived only in personal terms. For to experience reality as making demands on us antecedent to choice, and therefore regardless of our intentions, is to experience it, not simply as the object of our own intending and relative to us, but itself as intending us and absolutely other. It is to experience our involvement with the other-than-self as more than one with something determinate and manipulable; it is to experience ourselves as involved with an initiative which transcends our own, a determining source which addresses us and expects an answer. It is to be conscious of the other as that to which our very actuality as subjects, our own intentional life, is essentially a response; as that to which we ourselves are relative. It is, in short, to be conscious of the other as *You*, and of ourselves as constituted by a relation to You. In other words, my very being as I is an intention of You, an interest in You as the ground of my life. My life, what I do, the commitments I make are all rationally grounded only to the extent that they are regulated by this interest, informed by this intention, are determinate embodiments of *our* relationship. What is done must be *our* doing, not mine alone. Any actualizations of me must be actualizations in which You also are taken into account, in which You also have a part. To be grounded, they must be determinate realizations of *us*, determinate realizations of community. In this sense, the interest in You which I am is an interest in community. The transcendent end to which I in my very reality as subject am ordered is the continual achievement of a common life with You. The exigencies which confront me prior to choice are the exigencies of a personal relationship which transcends any of its particular realizations and, as the inclusively real, is the Value presupposed by any value and the basis for judging all of them. Nothing has final worth except as contributing, directly or indirectly, to a determinate realization of this ultimate relationship.

Thus, in addition to that intention of You which I am by nature, living morally requires my personal intention to act accordingly, my choice to embody in my life and actions that relationship which constitutes me a person in the first place. It is this intention, this original choice, which gives rise to distinctively moral inquiry and sustains it once it has arisen. Without such a choice, the moral question which is posed by my nature as subject is brushed aside, and those interests which make up my nature as object are given free rein, with the strongest taking over when they happen to conflict. This means that moral deliberation, which is integral to living morally and, as something I freely engage in, is already a determination of myself as response to You, presupposes moral commitment—the commitment to realize that to which my nature as person already commits me. The moral commitment is thus a kind of reduplication in my intentional life of that original intention which I am. It is a matter of freely adopting the objective interest, i.e., the interest in You, which is my nature as subject, as my final standard of evaluation. Since this interest is the ground of my intentional life and is presupposed in the rational pursuit of anything else, its adoption as final standard cannot be rationally questioned. To deliberate about committing myself to it is already to misconceive it, i.e., to conceive it as being on the level of the interests which I have as object and not as that to which those interests themselves are relative.[15] The moral commitment, therefore, is not a matter of deliberation but of self-appropriation.[16] It is a matter of choosing to be in the conduct of my life what I am antecedent to choice and by nature—a response to You. It is making my own the task of every man which, in the classic phrase, is to become what he is. Commitment to this task is categorically imperative for anyone aware of himself as an I. A person can indeed refuse to make it, and even try to rationalize his refusal, but he cannot do so without paying the price of experiencing his consequent life as lacking grounds and at odds with his own being. The only alternative to that act of self-appropriation which I call the moral commitment are groundlessness and alienation—which is to say, there are no real or rational alternatives. To prefer them is to prefer nothing to something, the realization of non-being to the incarnation of being. This is why a man can fail as a man. For, since man is a continually-to-be-realized community of persons in relation, being a man is never mere matter of fact, but always a matter of choice.

It should be clear by now why I said that the moral order has its roots in the essentially interpersonal structure of human existence. The moral order is that order of exigencies which stems from the fact that to be a person, an I, is to be in relation with You. No act can be an authentic realization of myself unless it is at the same time a realization of this relationship. To attempt otherwise, to posit myself in isolation from You, is to be isolated in my actions from my own being. It is to realize myself, not as I, but as object in the world, an object among objects; to subordinate my intentional life to what is relative and subordinate to it. Since no object—and that includes myself as object—can rationally ground my intention of it, committing myself to objects apart from You is to embark on a groundless course and to empty my life of meaning. Right and wrong are reduced to the level of technology. For, only what transcends my reality as subject can ground my life as subject. Only what is an end prior to choice can ground my choice of ends. Only what is unconditioned by my intentions can be regulative of those intentions. And You alone are all that. Right and wrong in the moral sense are inconceivable apart from the requirements of that transcendental relation to You which I am.

It should also be clear from all that has been said how this interpersonal structure of human existence grounds the possibility of objective judgments of moral value. For, like any judgment of value, a moral judgment is about the relation between one objective content and another. The determinate actualization of a subject is being appraised in terms of its relation to the achievement of community. The intended end, a genuinely common life, is functioning as the standard for evaluating a particular choice. The question is whether or not the choice contemplated is, as a specific commitment of the subject, consistent with such an end and a realization of it. If it is, it is right; if not, it is wrong. In either case, the consistency or inconsistency which is affirmed is something independent of the judger's whims and completely objective. And the judgment will be objectively true if what is affirmed is actually the case.

However, unlike judgments of value in which the standard of evaluation is something relative to man's intentional life, moral judgments are objective in a further sense. For, the moral standard is one to which man's own intentional life, his aims, interests, and purposes themselves are all relative. As the end to which all men are in their life as subjects ordered prior to choice, it is an absolute standard rationally binding on all alike—and this regardless of their empirical aims and purposes, attractions, and aversions. A judgment based on the moral standard, therefore, if it is true at all, will be true for all. What is morally right or wrong is universally so.

Here, finally, we have a rational way for coping with conflicts of interest. That way is inevitably the way of communication, of coming to common and mutually acceptable terms. For, since our empirical interests have objective worth only as subordinate to and regulated by our interest as persons (our interest in community), it is in the ultimate interest of neither party to a conflict of interest simply to have his own way. Or better, to put it positively: in the case of genuinely conflicting interests, the real interest of each party lies in coming to terms with the other, i.e., in finding out what modification of his project would render its realization something acceptable to the other. For the interest which constitutes us persons requires that no action determining our common world be taken unilaterally, that every determination of that world be something in which we both concur. Not only can our common world not be determined in incompatible ways; no determination of it can be of final worth to anyone if it cuts him off from the other-as-You.

In this light, justice in the concrete is the product of communication. It is impossible of achievement unless intended by both sides to any dispute. For a genuinely common project must be framed and undertaken in common. More, then, is required for settling conflicts of interest than the common nature of the disputants. That "more" is the moral commitment. Reason can replace force as the shaper of the world only if each of us is more interested in maintaining and developing a common life than in simply having his own way. If that day seems far off, it is not because there is no transcendent interest which can serve as final standard for judging what is really worth doing, but because we have not committed ourselves to its realization. In the last analysis, the reason we remain at odds with one another is that we are still in our hearts at odds with ourselves.

NOTES

1. See, for example, Joseph Margolis, *Values and Conduct* (New York: Oxford University Press, 1971), especially his concluding remarks on p. 212. When D. Z. Phillips and H. O. Mounce argue for the possibility in principle of "permanent radical moral disagreement" in "On Morality Having a Point" (*Philosophy* 50, No. 154 [1965], 308-19), they are making the same point.

2. One recent and lonely advocate of this position is Henry Veatch in *For an Ontology of Morals* (Evanston: Northwestern University Press, 1971). However, because of its exclusive reliance on the potency–act schema of Aristotle, I do not think that his ontology is equal to the task.

3. See the example of the Catholic housewife and the scientific rationalist arguing about birth control in the above-cited article of Phillips and Mounce. Their conflicting positions presuppose, and are supported by, different moral traditions, but (say the authors) there is no evidence independent of such traditions for deciding between them.

4. As Kai Nielsen finally admits in "Why Should I Be Moral?" (*Methodos* 15, Nos. 59-60 [1963], 275-306), it all depends on the sort of person I am and the circumstances I find myself in. He hastens to assure us, however, that there are enough social pressures around to keep most of us moral most of the time.

5. For example, by people like Herbert Marcuse, on the one hand, and B. F. Skinner, on the other.

6. See, for example, his *Experience and Nature* (New York: Dover, 1958), p. 135.

7. This point is made very well by John Macmurray in *Persons in Relation* (London: Faber, 1961), pp. 40-42.

8. Cf. Bernard Lonergan, *Method in Theology* (New York: Herder, 1972), pp. 34-41. That I am also indebted to John Rawls will be clear from what follows. See especially Chapter VII of *A Theory of Justice*: "Goodness as Rationality" (Cambridge: The Belknap Press of Harvard University Press, 1971).

9. Margolis fails to recognize this when he includes what he calls "appreciative judgments" under the heading of value judgments (*op. cit.*, p. 21), and then reduces moral judgments to appreciative judgments (*op. cit.*, p. 208). He forgets that a judgment is essentially the answer

to a question and that there are different kinds of judgments, not first of all because there are different kinds of predicates, but because there are different kinds of questions, questions which *intend* different things.

10. This is the temptation underlying ethical naturalism. A version of such naturalism, worked out in opposition to the contemporary move toward non-cognitivism in ethics, is found in Philippa Foot, "Moral Beliefs," *Proceedings of the Aristotelian Society*, 59 (1958-1959), 83-104.

11. Kai Nielsen (*art. cit.*, Sect. IV) dismisses the idea of normative human nature as simply an out-dated Greek idea (he prefers Sartre's notion that man has no essence), and we have already seen (n. 4) how far that takes him.

12. A good example of this sort of analysis can be found in Joseph Margolis, *op. cit.*, pp. 31-35; also in Section IV of Nielsen's "Why Should I Be Moral?"

13. John Macmurray, *op. cit.*, p. 38.

14. As Tillich puts it: "Man is able to ask because he is separated *from*, while participating *in*, what he is asking about" (*The Courage To Be* [New Haven: Yale University Press, 1952], p. 48).

15. It is this misconception, it seems to me, which underlies and vitiates most of the discussion about the so-called Ultimate Question in moral philosophy, to wit: Why be moral? See, for example, Paul W. Taylor, *Problems of Moral Philosophy* (Encino, Calif.: Dickenson, 1972), pp. 483-96.

16. Readers of Lonergan will recognize my indebtedness to him for the way I use this term here, as well as for the general direction of this paper.